When Your Teenager's Actions Cross the Line

A Guide for Parents of Youth with Sexual Behavior Problems

Rick Morris

Disclaimer

The information contained in this book is intended to serve as a guide for parents dealing with teens who have sexual behavior problems. While every effort has been made to ensure the accuracy and reliability of the information provided, this book is not a substitute for professional legal or medical advice, diagnosis, or treatment.

Suppose your teen is facing legal issues due to their sexual behaviors. In that case, consulting with qualified legal professionals is crucial to understanding the specific laws and regulations that may apply in your jurisdiction. Legal consequences can be severe, and only a qualified attorney can provide the advice you need.

Similarly, consult a qualified healthcare provider for diagnosis and treatment if your teenager is experiencing mental health issues or other medical conditions. A licensed mental health counselor or medical doctor should be consulted for a thorough evaluation and appropriate treatment plan tailored to your teen's needs.

By reading this book, you acknowledge that it is not a substitute for professional advice. The author and publisher disclaim any liability arising directly or indirectly from using the information in this book.

Copyright @ 2023 by Rick Morris
All Rights Reserved
First Edition, 2023

No part of this book may be reproduced, stored in a retrieval system, or transmitted in any form or by any means, electronic, mechanical, photocopying, recording, or otherwise, without the prior written permission of the publisher, except in the case of brief quotations embodied in critical articles and reviews.

ISBN: Printed: 979-8-9881856-6-6   eBook: 979-8-9881856-2-8

Youtube: @Tools4TeensandParents
www.sayhelp.net
www.tools4teens.net

CONTENTS

	Introduction	1
1	Assisting Your Adolescent and Supporting the Victim	5
2	Moving Forward and Finding Hope	9
3	12 Steps for Parents	15
4	Sexual Behavior Between Siblings	23
5	The Potential Consequences of Sex Offender Registration	33
6	Exploring the Reasons Behind Sexually Inappropriate Behavior	37
7	Family Dynamics and Effects	43
8	Safety Planning and Oversight	49
9	Treatment Programs and Their Approach	61
10	Protecting Your Teen in the Online World	73
11	Navigating Dating and Personal Relationships	77
12	Communicating After the News	81
13	Final Thoughts	97

Appendix

A	Parents with a history of prior sexual abuse	99
B	Glossary of Terms	103
C	Know Your Labels (FAQ)	109
D	Recommended Books	111
E	Youth Needs and Progress Scale	113
F	References & Resources	115

Introduction

When Your Teenager's Actions Cross the Line: A Guide for Parents of Youth with Sexual Behavior Problems

Welcome to **When Your Teenager's Actions Cross the Line: A Guide for Parents of Youth with Sexual Behavior Problems.** This book is designed to provide parents and caregivers of teens struggling with sexually inappropriate behaviors with the guidance, information, and resources to navigate this difficult journey. Discovering your teen's involvement in sexual behavior problems can be overwhelming and confusing. I hope to offer you a clear and compassionate roadmap that will help you understand the situation's difficulties and empower you to provide the best possible support for your child.

As a parent, I recognize the concerns and fears you may be facing. I want you to know that you're not alone on this journey. I've worked with many youths and their families dealing with the effects of finding that your child has acted out sexually. It will get better; you are not alone. Now you are part of a group of families whose lives have been changed, but many say after the journey, changed for the better.

My goal is to arm you with knowledge, equip you with tools, and instill a sense of hope as you navigate the challenges ahead. In the following chapters, we will address various topics, including understanding the legal system, addressing sibling sexual abuse, communicating effectively with your teen, creating a healthy living plan, and finding the right professionals to support your family. We'll share real-life examples and verbatim conversations to help you connect with the content and gain practical insights.

Whether your teen's situation involves a first-time offense or a more complex situation, this book is tailored to meet your needs. By using this resource, you'll gain a deeper understanding of the underlying factors contributing to your teen's behavior and discover practical steps you can take to promote healing, rehabilitation, and a hopeful future. I hope this book provides support and guidance during this challenging time and helps you navigate the challenges ahead with compassion, understanding, and resilience.

Navigating the challenges of parenting a teenager can be a daunting task, but what happens when their actions veer into unfamiliar and concerning territory? This guide is a compassionate and informative resource that delves into the sensitive topic of adolescent sexual behavior problems.

Written with empathy and expertise, I hope this guide will provide parents with a roadmap for understanding, supporting, and guiding their teenagers through these challenging circumstances. Based on the latest research, professional insights, and real-life stories, this guide offers practical strategies, valuable advice, and a sense of reassurance for parents facing the complexities of their teen's sexual behavior problems.

I'll cover the following topics and more in this guide:

Supporting your teen – Parents need to understand that their child's behavior is not their fault; they can still love and support their child while holding them accountable for their actions. It is crucial to seek assistance from qualified professionals who can help your teen understand the seriousness of their behavior and guide them toward rehabilitation.

Supporting the victim – Parents should remain conscious of the consequences of their child's actions on the victim and their family. Recognizing the harm caused, showing genuine remorse, and extending support to the victim and their family are essential steps. This is especially true when the behavior has affected a sibling. Additionally, parents can collaborate with their children to make reparations and implement measures to prevent any future harm.

Emotional health of parents/caregivers – Acknowledging the emotional toll this situation can take on parents and caregivers is essential. You may experience feelings of guilt, shame, anger, and confusion. It's essential to prioritize self-care, seek support from trusted friends and professionals, and find healthy coping methods.

Likelihood of reoffending – Studies have revealed that most juvenile offenders involved in sexual misconduct do not continue these behaviors into adulthood. This is particularly evident when they receive suitable treatment and support, with active involvement from their parents and caregivers in rehabilitation.

Impact of sex offender registration – Teenagers subject to sex offender registration may face substantial and enduring repercussions, such as difficulty attending school, finding employment, housing, and social support. Understanding the potential implications of registration and working with legal professionals to minimize its impact is essential.

Pro-social and protective factors – Parents can play a critical role in promoting pro-social and protective factors in their child's life. This includes building strong relationships with their child, encouraging positive peer relationships, promoting healthy attitudes towards sexuality, and participating in community activities that promote positive youth development.

Identifying specific risk factors – It's important to identify specific risk factors that may contribute to a teenager's engagement in sexual misconduct and develop a safety plan to mitigate these risks. This plan may entail increased supervision, monitoring of online activity, and engagement in treatment and support services.

This guide is designed as a quick resource for parents, providing clear sections and action items to assist you in navigating this challenging situation. Feel free to jump around the chapters as needed; don't feel like this is a book you must read cover to cover. The end of this guide also offers a list of helpful resources for parents to find additional support, information, and guidance. You'll also find guided conversation scripts for the more complex discussions.

| 1 |

Assisting Your Adolescent and Supporting the Victim

Discovering that your adolescent child has engaged in sexually inappropriate behavior can devastate parents and caretakers. It's challenging to reconcile your love and concern for your child with the potential harm they may have caused. However, it's essential to remember that your child's behavior does not reflect your parenting or family beliefs.

Exposure to pornography, peer pressure, and trauma are all factors that can contribute to adolescent sexual misconduct. To address these issues, one of the crucial steps parents can take is to seek assistance from qualified professionals to help their children comprehend the seriousness of their behavior and work toward rehabilitation.

For a parent or caregiver of a child who has engaged in sexually inappropriate behavior, it is essential to acknowledge the harm caused to the victim and their family. While this can be an emotional and challenging process, prioritizing the victim's well-being is crucial. Offering support and necessary resources to the victim and their family becomes a significant responsibility in this situation.

Listening to the victim and their family without judgment or defensiveness is vital, as is the ability to recognize the consequences of their child's behavior and express genuine remorse for the harm caused. Parents can also work with their teen to make amends and take preventative measures. This may include writing an apology letter, engaging in restorative justice programs, and seeking treatment and support.

However, it is crucial to approach this process with sensitivity and respect for the victim's needs and wishes, making sure their well-being is a top priority throughout. You may consider legal and protective measures such as restraining orders, safety planning, supervision, and monitoring. The National Child Traumatic Stress Network has created a resource guide for families of child sexual abuse victims. This may involve individual or family therapy, group therapy, and specialty treatment programs.

The *National Sexual Violence Resource Center* offers a complete guide when sexual abuse is identified. Resources for the child doing the inappropriate behavior and the child being harmed. Additionally, it is critical to have open and honest conversations with your child about their behavior, its impact on others, and the potential consequences. Striking a balance between accountability and support can be challenging. Still, it is essential to hold your child accountable for their actions while also recognizing their worth and capacity for growth.

Prioritizing self-care and seeking support from reliable peers and professionals is essential for parents dealing with such difficult situations. The American Psychological Association's article on supporting children who have engaged in risky sexual behaviors can provide valuable advice on managing emotions and responses effectively. Moreover, the National Child Traumatic Stress Network's guide offers resources for parents to address sexual abuse with their children and find the necessary support and assistance they need.

> *So, what should a parent do if their child has crossed the line with sexual behavior against a family member or a close friend?*

Suppose a parent discovers that their child has engaged in sexually inappropriate behavior with a family member or a close friend of the family. In this distressing scenario, immediate action is imperative to safeguard the safety of all individuals involved.

Dealing with your teen and his sexually inappropriate behavior requires a multifaceted strategy that includes legal, mental health, and community-based resources and support. Parents and their teen can navigate this difficult situation and move toward a healthier, more positive future by working together and focusing on positive change.

Parents should collaborate with their teen and professionals to create a rehabilitation and community reintegration plan while emphasizing healthy attitudes and behaviors toward sex and relationships. It is also critical for parents to concentrate on creating a supportive and nurturing home environment, as well as seeking out positive role models and community resources.

The first and most crucial step is ensuring the victim's safety and providing them with access to necessary support and resources. This may entail reporting the behavior to law enforcement or child protective services and arranging for appropriate medical or mental health assistance for the victim.

Parents must also grasp the legal process and the potential consequences for their child. Collaborating with legal professionals is essential to ensure the best possible outcome for their child and all parties affected. Seeking appropriate legal advice and representation for their child is critical, as they may face legal charges and consequences due to their behavior. This could include being listed on a sex offender registry, which could significantly impact your teen's future opportunities and relationships.

During this challenging time, prioritizing the well-being and safety of all individuals involved should be the utmost concern for parents. Taking immediate and appropriate action can help address the situation effectively and work towards healing and resolution for everyone impacted.

Getting your teen into therapy or counseling is a valuable resource to address the underlying factors that lead to inappropriate behavior.

This approach can help your teen develop healthy coping skills and attitudes toward sex and relationships.

Additionally, family therapy will likely be expected for handling any family dynamics or issues that could have contributed to your teen's behavior. Family therapy can play a significant role in strengthening communication and relationships among family members.

Further, seeking out support groups or other resources designed for families of individuals who have acted out sexually can be valuable. These tools create a safe and supportive environment for parents to connect with others who have experienced similar situations, offering guidance and advice on navigating this complex and challenging circumstance.

Parents should actively engage with their children to cultivate positive attitudes and behaviors regarding sex and relationships. This involves educating and raising awareness about healthy sexuality, consent, and the importance of respecting boundaries.

On a similar note, parents should concentrate on creating a supportive and nurturing home setting for the family to assist them in developing resilience and healthy coping skills. Creating clear boundaries and expectations, building regular routines and rituals, and fostering good communication and relationships within the family are all a part of this journey.

Another critical factor during this time is to help your teen identify positive role models and community resources, such as mentors, coaches, or faith-based groups. Outside the family, these positive influences can reinforce healthy attitudes and behaviors and provide a sense of belonging and support.

Finally, dealing with sexually inappropriate behavior by your teen can be a complex and emotional process for parents. Parents and their teenagers can manage this difficult situation and move towards a healthier and more positive future by taking proactive steps to prevent sexual abuse and exploitation and working together to address any existing issues. It is critical to seek appropriate resources and support and prioritize both the parents and the teen's well-being and long-term success.

| 2 |

Moving Forward and Finding Hope

The Section is for the Youth who acted out.

Understanding your Inappropriate Behavior and Finding Hope for the Future

Being investigated or arrested for sexually inappropriate behaviors can be tough to understand. It can be hard to know why you acted the way you did, and it can feel like you're alone in your struggles. But we want you to know that you're not alone and that there is hope for a better future.

First of all, it's important to understand that there are many reasons why someone might behave inappropriately sexually. It could be related to a difficult home life, past trauma, or other issues you may not know about. You are not alone; other teens have successfully gotten through this.

However, it is your responsibility to work with your parents and your treatment provider to understand what led to your behavior and work towards positive change.

You might feel like you're the only one who has ever behaved this way, but that's not true. Many teenagers struggle with sexually inappropriate behavior, and it's more common than you might think.

When Your Teenager's Actions Cross the Line

You are not alone in your struggles, and there is help available to you.

Working with your parents and your treatment provider will help you to understand why you behaved inappropriately and work towards a better future. Your treatment provider can help you learn new skills for coping with difficult emotions, as well as ways to promote healthy relationships and respect for others.

It won't be an easy road, but we believe in you. You are a teen who made a mistake, and you have the power to make things right. You can learn from this experience and grow into a better, stronger person.

Sometimes teenage boys act inappropriately sexually because they don't know how to handle their emotions or express themselves in a healthy way. Other times, teenage boys may act out sexually because they have experienced trauma or abuse in their past.

Some teenage boys may struggle with other things like anger, depression, anxiety, ADHD, or some other type of impulsive problem. Peer pressure or the desire to fit in can also lead teenage boys to engage in sexually inappropriate behavior. Teenage boys who struggle with addiction or substance abuse may also be more likely to engage in sexually inappropriate behavior.

Let's face it: you have likely been experiencing many different thoughts and feelings with your changing body and puberty. It's important to understand that there is never an excuse for behaving inappropriately sexually, but it can be helpful to understand some of the reasons why this behavior might occur.

Remember, your mistakes do not define you. With the help of your parents and your treatment provider, you can work toward a positive future and learn healthy ways to cope with difficult emotions and situations.

For the Parent or Caregiver

Moving Forward with Hope and Resilience

As a parent, you have faced a tough journey alongside your teen, navigating through the challenges of their inappropriate behavior. This experience must have been overwhelming, emotionally taxing, and undoubtedly difficult for you and your entire family. However, amidst the difficulties you have also discovered profound insights about your teen, yourself, and the strengths that bind your family together.

As you and your teen move forward, focus on hope and resilience. Remember, your teen's inappropriate behaviors do not define who they are. Your teenager is still the same individual with unique strengths, talents, and potential. Your teen can overcome past behaviors and build a positive future with proper support, guidance, and resources.

An essential step in moving forward is to partner with your treatment provider and the treatment plan. The measurable goals and objectives established with the treatment provider can help you and your teenager track progress and ensure that the treatment plan is effective. Celebrate your teenager's achievements, no matter how small they may seem. Recognize their efforts and remind them of the positive changes they have made.

A comprehensive treatment plan, including a Healthy Living Plan, should be well-structured and include measurable goals, objectives, and interventions. It should focus on developing new coping skills, addressing underlying issues, and reducing the risk of future incidents. It is essential to monitor progress regularly and adjust the treatment plan as needed to ensure that it is effective.

Continue being open and honest in your communication with your teen. Let them know that you love and support them and that you are there to help them through this process. Encourage them to express their thoughts and feelings and help them develop healthy coping skills to deal with stress and challenging situations.

As a family, consider participating in support groups or family therapy sessions to strengthen your relationships and build a support system. Reach out to community resources and organizations for additional guidance and support. Treatment and therapy can be incredibly effective in helping teenagers to understand their behavior, develop new coping skills, and prevent future incidents. Treatment providers can work with the legal system to ensure that the teenager receives the best possible care while also complying with legal requirements.

Remember that no two situations are the same and that each family will have unique challenges and experiences. However, by sharing our collective knowledge and expertise in this field, we hope to make this process more transparent for parents and caregivers facing this difficult situation.

We have covered a wide range of topics, from the legal implications of sexual acting out to the emotional toll that it can take on both the teenager and their family. We have discussed the role of therapy and treatment in helping your teen to understand their behavior and to develop new coping skills, as well as the importance of a healthy living plan to prevent future incidents.

One of the most critical messages throughout this book is that there **IS** hope. Teenagers who have acted out sexually inappropriately can and do move past their behavior and go on to lead healthy, productive lives. However, it takes a robust support system of parents, caregivers, therapists, and treatment providers to make this happen.

Parents and caregivers must remain patient and supportive throughout the recovery process. It may take time for your teen to fully understand their behavior and develop new coping skills, and setbacks may occur along the way. However, with the proper support and treatment, your teen can move past their behavior and lead a healthy and productive life.

Finally, while dealing with this situation may be difficult, it does not define your teen or the family. By working together, seeking help, and remaining hopeful, a better future can be achieved for everyone involved.

| 3 |

12 Steps for Parents

The following steps, adapted from the Alcoholics Anonymous program, can provide structure and guidance for parents and families after sexual abuse has been identified:

1. Acknowledge your child's inappropriate sexual behavior and recognize the problem's magnitude.
2. Believe in the existence of people who can help your family.
3. Allow those who understand the problem to assist your family.
4. Stop blaming others and admit the seriousness of the problem.
5. Admit what your child has done wrong and the harm caused to others.
6. Be ready to do whatever it takes to help your child change.
7. Be willing to examine your own history of victimization and abusive behaviors.
8. Recognize what you can change about yourself and your family and work on changing them.
9. Recognize signs and situations that put your child at risk and seek help when needed.
10. Acknowledge the harm caused by your child's behavior and be willing to help them make amends.
11. Stay aware of your child's problems and take necessary precautions to prevent harm to others.
12. Help other parents of teens with similar problems by sharing your experiences and insights.

These steps can help you adopt positive and healthy attitudes about your teen's behavior and treatment. They can also support and enhance the treatment process for your teen.

It is crucial to maintain an environment of calm and non-judgmental open communication, even when the discussions are difficult and emotionally charged. Keep in mind that anger and confrontation usually lead to defensiveness and withdrawal. Understand that your teen is probably scared and confused, even if they do not show it. They need reassurance that they are loved and supported despite their actions and that they can change and grow from this experience.

One of the first steps you will need to take is to get a professional assessment of your child's behavior and needs. This assessment will help you understand the problem's scope and what kind of treatment and counseling might be necessary. It's important to seek professionals who specialize in working with adolescents with sexual behavior problems, as they will be best equipped to assess and guide you and your teen through this challenging journey.

In addition, finding a supportive community, such as a parent support group, can be immensely helpful. This can be a place where you can share your feelings, concerns, and experiences with others who are going through the same or similar situations. This sense of community can be a source of great strength and consolation. It's important to remember that you are not alone and that many parents have faced and successfully navigated similar circumstances.

Throughout this process, it's critical to maintain open lines of communication with your teen. Let them know that you're there for them and that they can talk to you about anything. While it may be difficult, avoid expressing anger or judgment as much as possible; this can push your teen away and make them less likely to open up. Instead, approach them with love, compassion, and understanding, reassuring them that while their actions are problematic, you know that they can change and grow.

Beyond understanding what normal sexual behavior in adolescence looks like and how to identify potential signs of abusive or inappropriate behavior, there are other important aspects to consider.

Teach about Safe Sex:
If your teenager becomes sexually active, it's essential they understand how to protect themselves against sexually transmitted infections (STIs) and unwanted pregnancies.

Know the Signs of Abuse:
Educate yourself and your teenager about the signs of sexual abuse and unhealthy relationships, such as coercion, manipulation, extreme jealousy, and physical violence. Make sure your teen knows they can come to you if they or a friend are experiencing these signs.

Support:
If you suspect your teen has been involved in abusive or inappropriate sexual behavior, either as a victim or perpetrator, seek professional help immediately. Consult with a child psychologist, counselor, or other mental health professionals who specialize in adolescent behavior.

Remember, it's okay to seek outside help. You don't have to navigate this alone, and there are many resources available for parents and teenagers dealing with these challenging topics.

Empowering Parents/Caregivers: Providing Support and Guidance

Discovering that their teenage child has been arrested for sexually inappropriate behaviors can be an overwhelming and distressing experience for a parent or guardian. It may evoke feelings of shock, devastation, shame, guilt, and anger, as they grapple with not only the present situation but also concerns about their child's future.

Shame is a common and natural emotion experienced by parents in this challenging situation. They may internalize feelings of failure, believing their child's behavior reflects poorly on their parenting. However, it's essential for parents to recognize that these feelings do not define them as individuals or as parents.

Dealing with shame can be addressed by confiding in a trusted friend, family member, or doctor about their emotions. Opening up about their feelings and experiences with others who have gone through similar circumstances can be cathartic, providing a safe space without fear of judgment. Joining support groups specifically designed for parents of teenagers who've engaged in sexually inappropriate behaviors can also be beneficial, as it offers a supportive community to navigate this challenging journey together.

Anger is another normal feeling that some parents experience in such a situation. They might feel anger towards their child for hurting someone or angry at the system for arresting their teen. While it's natural to feel anger, parents need to channel that emotion in a positive way rather than lashing out at their child or others.

Managing anger constructively is crucial for both the well-being of the parents and the family dynamic. Seeking support through therapy or counseling can be beneficial in learning healthy coping mechanisms and effective communication strategies. By addressing their anger in a positive manner, parents can create a more conducive environment for understanding, healing, and supporting their child through this challenging time.

Parents should keep in mind that their feelings and actions can significantly impact their teen's well-being and the pace of their recovery. If parents are struggling with their emotions, they might inadvertently make their child feel more isolated and unsupported, hindering their progress. Children are sensitive to their parent's feelings, and if they perceive that their parents are overwhelmed by shame or anger, it can intensify their feelings of isolation and detachment. Therefore, it is crucial for parents and caregivers to address their emotions effectively so that they can better support and assist their children during challenging times. By managing their feelings well, parents create a more nurturing environment for their children's healing and growth.

Parents should create an environment of trust and open communication to support their teen effectively. This means listening to their child's point of view without passing judgment or assigning blame, providing unwavering support and encouragement for positive changes, and working with their teen's treatment team to address the underlying issues that contributed to the inappropriate behavior.

Additionally, parents should seek to educate themselves about the challenges associated with sexually inappropriate behavior and how to support their child through the healing process best. They can do this by attending classes, reading relevant books or articles, or seeking expert guidance.

Understanding that their teen's healing is a gradual process that requires time and effort is crucial for parents. It's not uncommon for teens to experience relapses or setbacks during treatment, which may trigger feelings of anger or discouragement for parents. However, it is vital for parents to remain patient and supportive while holding their children accountable for their actions and growth.

In the end, the best thing parents can do is to take care of themselves and their children. This involves taking care of themselves, asking for help from others when needed, and recognizing their own limits. It's perfectly okay for parents to get help for their mental health, as this can benefit both themselves and their children in the long run.

Identifying Specific Risk Factors

Identifying particular risk factors can help avoid future instances of sexually inappropriate behaviors and promote positive adolescent development. Individual risk factors, like being exposed to trauma, being alone, and having access to pornography, can be addressed with the help of trained experts. The U.S. Surgeon General recently identified Loneliness as a significant problem in our country. Post Covid and the many changes our families have undergone would suggest an intention to focus on family connection can help our teens.

It is essential to realize that every situation is different and that there is no one way to find specific risk factors that are drivers of your teen's sexual behaviors. Working with experienced experts, you can create a thorough evaluation plan and determine the precise variables contributing to their teens' behavior.

After figuring out the risk factors, parents and caretakers can work with experts to make a personalized therapy and prevention plan. Individual or family counseling, group therapy, and specialty therapeutic programs may be included.

It is also critical to encourage your teen consistently with open and honest dialogue to provide a secure and loving home setting. Some examples are setting clear limits, giving constant support and praise, and having open and honest conversations. Use this time to remind your teen that your job as a parent is to protect and teach which may not always match what your teen wants.

Finally, it is important to participate in continuous supervision to ensure that your child stays on course and progresses toward their objectives. Regular check-ins with experts who know what they're doing, more monitoring and tracking, and regular contact with your child's support team may occur.

Identifying specific risk factors can help avoid future sexual assault instances and promote positive adolescent development. Individual risk factors, such as trauma exposure, social isolation, and access to pornography, can be identified and addressed by parents and caretakers in collaboration with trained experts.

Addressing the Risk of Re-Offending: Supporting Rehabilitation and Prevention

Research shows that most young people who engage in sexually inappropriate behaviors tend not to repeat such actions. This is especially true if they receive the appropriate support and care, and when their parents and other caretakers actively participate in their rehabilitation process.

Early intervention and care are two pivotal steps in reducing the likelihood of repeated mistakes. A report from the Center for Sex Offender Management details that young individuals who engage in sexual misconduct do not frequently repeat such behavior. This underscores the significance of professional therapy programs and continuous support in promoting positive outcomes.

Promoting positive behavior and reducing the likelihood of inappropriate actions can be achieved through various actions taken by parents and caretakers. Building trusting and open connections with their children, educating them about healthy behavior and boundaries, and participating in neighborhood activities that support youth development are practical ways to accomplish this goal.

Last but not least, it's critical to understand that each situation is unique and that there is no one right method to assist individuals in getting better. To create a strategy that suits your child's requirements and circumstances, you must collaborate with qualified experts and attorneys.

| 4 |

Sexual Behavior Between Siblings

If you're reading this chapter, you're likely grappling with a devastating and complex emotional reality: one of your children has sexually abused their sibling. You might feel a whirlwind of emotions—anger, guilt, confusion, and profound sadness. These feelings can be overwhelming, and you may not know where to turn or what steps to take. This chapter aims to guide you through the treatment options for both the victim and the abuser in your family, offering a roadmap during this incredibly challenging time.

Definition of Sibling Sexual Abuse
Sexual abuse of siblings refers to any act or conduct of a sexual nature that takes place between siblings. This can vary from unwanted physical contact to more serious sexual assault. It is a sort of abuse that is frequently concealed, ignored, or misunderstood, but the repercussions of this kind of abuse are severe and long-lasting.

You may be wondering, "Is it abuse, or is it just curiosity?" Abuse refers to any sexual conduct that is characterized using compulsion, force, or manipulation. You may be tempted to brush it off as "kids being kids," but it is essential to realize that this issue requires quick action. You may feel as though you're the only one dealing with this challenge. However, it is essential to be aware that sexual assault between siblings occurs more frequently than most people believe.

The stigma and secrecy surrounding this topic frequently discourage families from seeking assistance, which can result in long-term harm for both the child who has been abused and the child who has done the abuse. When it is addressed sooner rather than later, there is a greater likelihood of rehabilitation and healing for everyone involved. Ignoring or downplaying the significance of the problem might contribute to the continuation of abusive behaviors and make it more challenging. You're not alone, and it's okay to seek help.

What Exactly Is Considered Sexual Abuse of a Sibling?

When you're a parent, one of the most challenging tasks you have is determining whether your child is engaging in age-appropriate curiosity or whether they are being abused. It's a line you never imagined you'd have to draw, and the obligation may make you feel like you're drowning in it.

If you have any lingering doubts, ask yourself the following:
- Was there a youngster who exhibited obvious discomfort or resistance?
- Were the siblings' ages quite different, or did they have very different power levels?
- Did the behaviors include any form of secrecy or threatening behavior?
- If any of these inquiries get the response "yes," it's pretty probable that you're dealing with abuse rather than simple curiosity.

Immediate Steps
To Begin With, Safety

Both children must be kept secure right away. Understand that temporary separation is not a punishment; instead, it is a necessary safety precaution that may cause you to feel conflicted between your obligations as a parent or caregiver for both of your children. This may require one of the children to spend some time with a relative or a close family friend. It's not an easy choice, but it needs to be made for the sake of the mental and physical health of both siblings.

The Reporting
The idea of going to the authorities might be quite scary. You may be worried about the consequences for both your family and your child who was responsible. However, you are responsible for understanding that reporting is frequently needed by law and is needed for the long-term health and safety of both children. Consult your local laws and regulations to have a better understanding of your responsibilities.

Legal Consequences
Because of the wide variety of potential legal consequences, you might want to speak with an attorney who is well-versed in family and juvenile law to gain an understanding of your situation. This is not only about following the law; it's also about being aware of the options that are available to help your family on its path to healing. See the American Bar Association at www.americanbar.org for more assistance.

Treatment for the Victim
Your child who has been abused is most certainly going through a range of feelings, some of which they may not completely understand or be able to articulate. Your support and understanding will go a long way in helping them. Individual counseling can provide a space that is both secure and confidential for one to investigate these feelings. When seeking a therapist, it is important to choose one that specializes in treating traumatic experiences, including sexual assault.

Treatment for the Abuser
You may be having difficulty processing how you feel about the child who was abusive. There are several normal responses one might have, including anger, disappointment, and confusion. Nevertheless, it is very necessary to transform these feelings into productive behavior. Your child needs specialist therapy from a therapist trained to address inappropriate behavior while understanding your whole teen. Your teen did not act out inappropriately just because they had sexual arousal. All teens go through puberty and the challenging developmental years and most don't exhibit these behaviors. Your treatment team should be able to address sexual behaviors while identifying deficits in self-image, communication, peer interactions,

etc. While building on your teen's strengths and reducing the deficits may have been a factor in the behavior.

Participation of the Family
You may wonder, "Where did we as a family go wrong?" It's a scary question, but the answer is usually confusing. Family counseling can help unpack these relationships by providing a controlled atmosphere in which each family member can communicate their thoughts and concerns in an organized manner.

Rebuilding Trust
Your family's trust in one another has been severely damaged. The process of rebuilding it is lengthy and complicated, and it demands the devotion of every family member. This process can be guided through family counseling, which can assist each member in expressing their thoughts and concerns in an atmosphere that is safe and organized.

Establishing Boundaries
To protect against further abuse, your family must develop some fresh guidelines and restrictions. This is a difficult process that requires open communication and frequently includes talks that are challenging. A therapist can help you work through this challenge and ensure everyone's continued safety and well-being as you move ahead.

Settling In with Your Thoughts and Emotions

Identification of the Signs and Behavioral Indicators of Abuse in the Offender

You, as a parent, are aware of your child's regular conduct, as well as their peculiarities and moods. Whenever there is a significant shift in the status quo, it should serve as a warning signal. It might be disturbing if you see that your kid is becoming increasingly secretive, such as by shutting doors when they never did so before or avoiding eye contact. These actions might be indications that the person is guilty or that they are aware of the wrongfulness of what they are doing.

You could also notice other changes, such as a sudden interest in sexual issues that go beyond what is considered age-appropriate, or perhaps they have begun demonstrating manipulative behavior with their sibling and other family members. Both are red flags that something might be wrong. These are warning signs that can't be disregarded in any way. It is distressing to consider the possibility that your child may have abused substances or other people, but recognizing the warning signals is the first step in addressing the problem and receiving the assistance that your family requires.

Warning Signs for Parents and Those Who Care for Children

Your instincts as a parent are one of the most powerful weapons at your disposal. A significant warning sign is thrown up if you notice that your youngster suddenly resists spending time alone with their sibling. They may have begun experiencing nightmares or showing indications of anxiousness, like wetting the bed or being too possessive of their belongings. These are some indications that something has taken place.

It is simple to have second thoughts, mainly when the repercussions are of such a significant kind. You may think you are overreacting or misreading the indicators presented to you. But go with your instincts; after all, you are the one who knows your children the best. If you get a strange feeling about anything, you're probably right.

If you are still unsure, you might want to explore getting the assistance of specialists who can give more objective direction. However, you should pay attention to your gut feelings since they are the first line of defense in protecting your children.

The IMPACT
Family Dynamics

The revelation that one of your children has engaged in sexually abusive behavior toward one of their siblings can have a ripple effect that affects your entire family. Your house undergoes a rapid transformation in terms of its psychological terrain. Your previous level of trust has been destroyed, your connections have been strained, and the dynamic of your family, as you previously knew, may forever be altered.

You may feel split between your natural impulse to protect the victim and your mixed feelings for your other children. This is a shared experience. Guilt may drag you down. You may lie awake at night thinking, "Where did I go wrong?" or "How did I not see this coming?" It is a psychological torment that no parent should be forced to go through, yet here you are, confronted with a circumstance that forces you to be more resilient than you ever imagined was possible.

You may also discover that your connection with your partner or other family members is strained because of the abuse. Everyone is going to have their unique emotional responses, and if people can't agree on how to handle the problem, it's going to drive a bigger wedge between them. It's a moment when your family must pull together.

The condition also applies to other children you may have at this time. Even if they don't completely understand what's going on, they can feel the tension and instability in the air. It's possible that they, too, may require emotional support and open communication to get through this challenging period.

Don't forget about your other children in the home. They may be identified as indirect victims. They may be spending many hours in the car going from appointment to appointment, waiting in the lobby while your teen goes to therapy. They also may have experienced loss of freedom and activities in the house with their siblings due to the history of what's taking place. In many situations these children don't even know what has occurred that made the changes.

The road to recovery and the re-establishment of family togetherness is a lengthy one that is littered with challenges. It will take the participation of trained professionals, honest communication, and a commitment from every family member to participate in the challenging work of healing. It won't be easy but remember that you don't have to do it alone. Help is available, but the first thing you need to do is acknowledge the impact the behavior has had on your family.

Legal Aspects
Specifications for Required Reporting

It is a terrible experience to come to terms with the possibility that you may have to turn in your child to the police. Your mind is probably racing with contradictory thoughts and feelings, such as worry for the future of your teen, anxiety about the health and happiness of both of your children and maybe even a sense of parental guilt or inadequacy on your part. These can be paralyzing, yet immediate action must be taken to ensure the safety and well-being of everyone concerned.

Different communities have different legal definitions of what constitutes sexual abuse between siblings. However, in a broader sense, it refers to any sexual act or behavior that takes place between siblings that involves coercion, manipulation, or force. This can range from unwelcome physical contact all the way up to more serious sexual assault. It is a kind of child abuse and, as such, is subject to rules in numerous countries that require mandatory reporting. The child doing the behavior may face legal consequences such as being required to undergo mandatory therapy, being sent to juvenile detention, or even, in extreme cases, being prosecuted as an adult with a felony if they are older than a certain age. Children can also be placed on the Sex Offender Registry, which can be devastating to the child but also to the victim and other family members. These outcomes vary based on the severity of the offense and the laws of the community.

The failure to disclose abuse can have serious repercussions, not just legally but also emotionally and mentally, for the abused child and the person who abused them. Abuse that is not reported has the potential to persist and worsen, causing the victim even more severe emotional distress and making the abuser's behavioral problems even more severe. In addition, the failure to disclose the abuse of a child is considered a criminal act in many places, and those who do so face the possibility of being fined or even imprisoned.

Immediately begin researching your area's laws to know your responsibilities. You will be required to follow the standards and procedures for reporting child abuse that are particular to your community, and you must do so very carefully. You may be compelled to report the abuse to the police or the local child protective services. The procedure will most certainly be challenging for your mental state. Still, it is a crucial step for maintaining the physical and legal integrity of your family unit and protecting your children.

You may want to consult an expert specializing in family law if you have any questions regarding the legal requirements or the procedure for reporting. They can direct you through the complicated legal process and explain what you might anticipate. Keep in mind that the purpose of reporting is not to punish the offender but rather to protect them and begin the process of intervening and healing them.

Moving Forward
Healing and Recovery

The road to recovery is long and winding, littered with emotional highs and lows at various points. You may have days when you feel like you're making progress and other days when you feel like you've gone ten steps backward. This is normal. It is essential to remember that healing is not a step-by-step process but a multi-step procedure that requires time, patience, and significant mental and emotional labor.

You are not engaged in a race; instead, you are navigating a marathon. There will be obstacles in the way, and that is normal. What is important is your determination to keep pushing ahead, even when it appears like there is no way out of the pain that you are experiencing. Your household will require ongoing psychotherapy, maybe for many years to come. In addition to this, you may need to evaluate the family's communication, safety precautions, and limits. It's a commitment for the long haul, but it's very necessary for the health and happiness of everyone involved.

Future Prevention

As you move on with the healing process, you will also need to consider how you might avoid similar situations in the future. Maintaining a state of constant attention is essential at this point. Your family's trust has likely been destroyed due to the abuse and restoring it will be a difficult and time-consuming journey that will demand constant participation from all family members.

Communication without barriers is essential. Establish a setting in which your children feel comfortable communicating their emotions, worries, and experiences with one another. Ensure that they are aware of the ideas of permission and limits and encourage them to communicate with you if they are unsure of their safety or experience discomfort.

In addition, you may be required to maintain a higher degree of control and oversight than you thought was needed in the past. It is not about intruding on the personal space of your children; instead, it is about looking out for their health and safety. Checking in with each other regularly as a family may be an effective method to check how everyone is doing emotionally and to spot any possible problems before they become more serious.

Ongoing Support

The healing process may take a long time and may have many highs and lows. Both children will require continuing assistance, maybe for many years to come. You should prepare for a long, challenging road, but you will make it. You are not alone.

Watch for Progress

You will want to see improvement, but you must remember that relapses are a natural and expected part of the recovery process. Regular check-ins with your therapist or counselor can help you realize what aspects of your treatment are successful and what aspects need some tweaking.

This is, without a doubt, going to be one of the most challenging experiences your family will ever go through. The psychological cost is enormous, but you don't have to face it alone if you don't want to. Getting help from professionals is necessary for the challenging healing process and regaining trust within your family. Take things one stride at a time, and always remember that you are not alone on this journey.

References and Resources
- American Psychological Association's Psychologist Locator: www.apa.org
- RAINN (Rape, Abuse & Incest National Network): www.rainn.org
- Association for the Treatment of Sexual Abusers: www.atsa.com
- American Association for Marriage and Family Therapy: www.aamft.org
- American Bar Association: www.americanbar.org

| 5 |

The Potential Consequences of Sex Offender Registration

Most teens involved in sexually inappropriate behaviors are not required to register on the national Sex offender registry. However, the families that have a teen who this ma may affect should be informed of the seriousness of the registry. The sex offender registry can profoundly impact a teenager's life, making it challenging for them to get a job, find housing, or receive community support. Recognizing the potential consequences of registration is crucial, and seeking guidance from legal professionals can aid in mitigating these effects.

One of the major hurdles is the stigma and discrimination that often accompany being listed on a sex offender registry. Teenagers may face difficulty integrating into society and accessing the assistance they require because many employers, landlords, and community members hold misconceptions about registered sex offenders and may even harbor fear towards them.

Along with social issues, being placed on the sex offender register may have legal and financial ramifications. Registered sex offenders may face more stringent legal restrictions, including residency, travel, and reporting requirements. Moreover, they might be obligated to pay fines and registration costs, which can be financially burdensome for teenagers and their families.

Parents and other caregivers should consult with lawyers to understand the specific effects of sex offender registration in their state and devise a plan to mitigate these consequences. This could involve working with advocacy groups, searching for legal assistance, and advocating for changes to licensure rules to minimize the impact on the teenager's life.

In simple terms, the Sex Offender Registration and Notification Act, also called SORNA, is part of a law called the Adam Walsh Child Protection and Safety Act. This law was made in 2006. The aim of SORNA is to keep track of people who committed sex crimes when they were teens.

According to this law, some teens who commit a sex crime must be listed in a sex offender registry. To be specific, these teens are those who:
- Were 14 or older when they committed the crime, and
- Have been found guilty of a sex crime that is as serious as, or more severe than, aggravated sexual abuse. Aggravated sexual abuse is a serious sex crime involving forcing someone into a sexual act.

Because these crimes are severe, these teens are in a tier III category under SORNA. This means they have specific rules to follow, like checking in person for a certain period. But the law doesn't say they must be on the registry forever without any conditions. They can be removed from the registry if they stay out of trouble for 25 years.

National Guidelines for Sex Offender Registration and Notification say that the sex crimes that put these teens on the registry are those like the crime of aggravated sexual abuse. In most cases, this involves forcing someone into a sexual act.

In 2011, additional guidelines for the Sex Offender Registration and Notification law came out. These guidelines gave places like states and cities the choice to show or not show information about teens found guilty of a sex crime on their local public website for sex offenders.

For instance, a city or state might set up a system to tell high school staff when a teen who committed a sex crime starts to go to their school. Or they might make a rule that the police, student services, or some other office at a local college get told when a teen who committed a sex crime starts classes or changes their registration information. Also, to keep people safe, there might be a system to tell certain groups or institutions that work to protect children or help worried parents. These groups could ask to know about teens who committed a sex crime and are on the registry.

Above all, prioritizing the teen's well-being is crucial, and helping them develop an identity separate from their past actions is essential. This may involve supporting them in building healthy relationships, engaging in positive activities with others, and advocating for their rights to access resources such as jobs and education. By focusing on their health and future growth, parents and caregivers can play a pivotal role in guiding teenagers toward a positive and fulfilling life beyond their past mistakes.

When Your Teenager's Actions Cross the Line

| 6 |

Exploring the Reasons Behind Sexually Inappropriate Behavior

Teenage sexual misbehavior is a complicated and frequently misconstrued problem. It is essential to know what may have led to a child's sexually inappropriate behavior. Researchers have found that sexual offenses by teenagers are more likely if they have been sexually abused, seen pornographic material, or if they have experienced some sort of violence or traumatic experience in childhood.

By understanding these factors, parents, caretakers, and experts can work collaboratively to prevent sexually inappropriate behavior in teens and offer support to those who have engaged in such conduct, helping them improve.

Sexual Abuse Victimization
Sexual maltreatment is one of the most critical risk factors for adolescent sexual offenses. Sexual abuse stress can affect a child's social, emotional, and cognitive growth, causing problems with relationships, self-regulation, and problem-solving. These challenges can add to the development of dysfunctional coping strategies, such as sexually improper behavior.

Exposure to Pornography
In recent years, the internet and social media have made pornography increasingly accessible, exposing many young people to sexually explicit content at a young age. This exposure to pornography has been associated with several detrimental effects, including an increased likelihood of engaging in sexually inappropriate behavior.

Studies have also found a link between pornography exposure and adolescent sexual misconduct.

Furthermore, research indicates that pornography may desensitize young individuals to sexual violence and hostility, potentially leading to the acceptance of these harmful behaviors. It is essential to recognize and address the impact of pornography on young people and take measures to promote healthy attitudes and behaviors regarding sex and relationships.

History of Trauma or Violence

Children who have experienced hurt or abuse may resort to unhealthy ways of coping with their feelings and sense of helplessness, including engaging in sexually inappropriate behavior. Additionally, exposure to stress and violence can desensitize young individuals to hostility and aggression, making them more prone to act similarly. Addressing these underlying issues and providing appropriate support and intervention is crucial in helping young people develop healthy coping mechanisms and prevent further harmful behaviors.

Unhealthy Peer Relationships

Unhealthy peer relationships can significantly influence a teen's behavior, primarily if they associate with peers who engage in criminal or sexually inappropriate conduct. The influence of negative peer groups can lead to higher chances of adolescents participating in similar behaviors. To mitigate this risk, parents, educators, and caregivers must encourage positive peer relationships and create an environment that promotes healthy social connections. By fostering supportive friendships and promoting pro-social activities, young individuals are more likely to make responsible choices and avoid engaging in harmful behaviors influenced by negative peer influences.

Mental Health Issues

Mental health conditions like depression, anxiety, or ADHD can impact a person's judgment, impulse control, and decision-making abilities, possibly contributing to risky behaviors. However, avoiding stigmatizing individuals with mental health issues as potential offenders is essential. By addressing mental health needs proactively, we can help young people navigate their challenges and promote positive behavioral outcomes.

Social Skill Problems

Young people who lack adequate social skills or find it challenging to make friends may be more susceptible to seeking comfort or validation through sexual activity. Engaging in sexual behavior can sometimes be perceived as a means of connection or acceptance, particularly if individuals struggle to establish meaningful relationships or feel socially isolated. Promoting activities that foster teamwork and cooperation can improve social interactions and reduce the likelihood of turning to sexual behavior as a substitute for emotional fulfillment.

Of course, it's important to understand that these risk factors do not inevitably lead to sexually inappropriate behavior in teenagers. Instead, they are factors that can increase the likelihood of such conduct. Many young people who have experienced sexual abuse, pornography exposure, or traumatic events do not engage in sexually inappropriate behavior. On the other hand, being aware of these risk factors can assist parents, caretakers, and experts in identifying young individuals at risk and providing them with appropriate support and intervention to address potential challenges effectively. By recognizing these factors, adults can play a crucial role in creating a supportive and nurturing environment for teenagers, promoting healthy behaviors, and preventing harmful conduct when possible.

Keeping Teens Safe

To prevent teenagers from engaging in harmful behaviors, a comprehensive plan that addresses fundamental risk factors, fosters healthy sexual development, and promotes positive relationships and communication is essential. Some effective methods for preventing adolescent sexual offenses include:

Dealing with Risk Factors

It is imperative to deal with the things that put teens at risk for sexual offenses, like sexual abuse, pornographic exposure, and a history of violence or trauma. This could include offering support and counseling to young people who have been victims of trauma or abuse and teaching them about healthy sexuality and relationships.

Promoting Healthy Sexual Development
Promoting healthy sexual development plays a crucial role in preventing inappropriate behavior in a sexual context. This approach involves teaching children about their bodies, relationships, and the importance of seeking permission in appropriate situations. It also includes fostering positive attitudes toward sexuality and relationships and offering support and guidance on issues related to sexual preference and gender identification.

Promoting Positive Relationships and Communication
To stop teens from committing sexual offenses, you must ensure they foster good relationships and can talk to each other. This could include encouraging healthy dialogue between parents and children and positive interactions between children and their classmates. It could also involve offering insight into subjects like dating and relationships.

Remember, teenagers who engage in sexually inappropriate behavior may not fully comprehend the consequences of their actions. Their cognitive and social development might not yet be mature enough to grasp the full impact of their behavior on others. This underscores the significance of implementing programs that promote accountability while offering opportunities for growth and learning.

As parents or caretakers of children who have participated in sexually improper behavior, it is critical to approach the situation with sensitivity. Also, an understanding of the underlying factors that led to the behavior. Seeking the assistance of skilled experts, such as specialized counselors, can be a helpful move in learning and resolving these issues.

Understanding the factors that lead to sexual misconduct by teens is a significant first step toward solving this difficult problem. Parents and other caretakers can help their children understand how wrong their actions were, take responsibility for them, and work toward recovery and healing by using a caring and thorough plan that includes the proper steps and help.

While these risk factors should not serve as excuses for the behavior of juveniles who engage in sexually inappropriate acts and face legal consequences, they underscore the importance of a comprehensive approach to prevention and treatment that addresses the underlying issues and promotes positive change.

Additionally, it's important to recognize that juveniles who have acted out sexually inappropriately are often victims of societal attitudes and stigmatization. The shame and social isolation accompanying a juvenile's arrest and subsequent legal proceedings can exacerbate underlying mental health issues and contribute to ongoing negative behaviors.

Therefore, parents, caregivers, and professionals need to approach juvenile sexual offending with a compassionate and non-judgmental mindset while still holding juveniles accountable for their actions.

Navigating Healthy Coping Skills: Action Steps for Parents and Teenagers Regarding Pornography Use

You'll first want to empower yourself and your child with knowledge about the potential detrimental impact of pornography on mental and sexual well-being. Seek valuable insights from credible sources, such as mental health professionals, sex educators, and organizations dedicated to preventing sexual violence.

Next, encourage healthy coping skills that do not involve the use of pornography. There are plenty of healthy and fun options, from exercise and meditation to creative activities and spending time with supportive friends and family.

Additionally, you'll want to create and enforce clear boundaries around internet and media use, including monitoring the use of electronic devices and installing filtering software that blocks access to pornography.

Of course, the true key in this situation is to foster open and honest communication between parents and teenagers about sex and relationships. This can include providing accurate sex education about consent, healthy relationships, and the potential risks of engaging in sexually inappropriate behavior. If you need assistance with this, don't hesitate to seek professional support if you or your child is struggling with the effects of pornography addiction or dependence. This can include therapy, counseling, and support groups.

Be sure also to encourage positive self-image and self-esteem. This can include promoting positive body image, self-love, and acceptance.

By following these steps, parents and teenagers can effectively reduce access to and dependence on pornography as a coping mechanism, fostering healthier attitudes and behaviors towards sex and relationships.

Parents must acknowledge that this process may require time and effort, and setbacks can happen. However, by maintaining open communication, working together, and seeking appropriate resources and support, parents and teenagers can successfully develop positive coping skills and attitudes toward sex and relationships. The journey towards a healthier perspective is worth both parents' and teenagers' commitment and dedication.

Parents must approach this issue with empathy, understanding, and a willingness to seek support and resources. By doing so, parents can play a critical role in helping their teen navigate the challenges of adolescence and build a healthy and fulfilling life.

| 7 |

Family Dynamics and Effects

Research has shown that exposure to domestic violence can significantly impact a child's psychological and emotional well-being and increase the risk of engaging in sexually inappropriate behavior later in life.

According to a study published in the Journal of Family Violence, children exposed to domestic violence are likelier to exhibit aggressive and violent behavior, experience depression and anxiety, and have difficulty forming healthy relationships later in life (Graham-Bermann & Perkins, 2010).

This is particularly true for boys, who may learn that violence and aggression are acceptable ways of expressing anger and frustration. This can lead to a greater risk of engaging in sexually inappropriate behavior and other forms of violence and aggression.

It is important for parents to recognize the potential impact of domestic violence on their child's psychological and emotional well-being and to seek out appropriate support and resources if necessary. This can include therapy, counseling, support groups, and involvement in community organizations focused on promoting healthy relationships and preventing domestic violence.

Parents should recognize that the effects of exposure to domestic violence may not always be immediately apparent. Children may not exhibit symptoms until later in life and may struggle to form healthy relationships and cope with the emotional and psychological effects of exposure to violence.

Therefore, parents must remain vigilant and proactive in addressing domestic violence and seek appropriate support and resources if necessary. By addressing the underlying issues and providing appropriate support and intervention, parents can help their child develop healthy coping skills and attitudes towards sex and relationships and reduce the risk of engaging in sexually inappropriate behavior later in life.

Effects of Previous Sexual Victimization

Research has shown that prior sexual victimization can significantly impact a teenager's sexual development and behavior and may increase the risk of engaging in sexually inappropriate behavior later in life.

According to a study published in the Journal of Interpersonal Violence, teenagers who have experienced sexual victimization may be more likely to engage in sexually inappropriate behavior and have difficulty developing healthy coping skills and attitudes toward sex and relationships (Reina & Loh, 2019).

This is particularly true for teenagers who have experienced sexual victimization at a young age, as they may struggle with shame, guilt, and confusion about their sexuality. This can lead to a greater risk of engaging in sexually inappropriate behavior later in life and other forms of sexual and interpersonal violence.

It is important for parents to recognize the potential impact of prior sexual victimization on their teenager's sexual development and behavior and to seek out appropriate support and resources if necessary. This can include therapy, counseling, support groups, and involvement in community organizations focused on promoting healthy attitudes toward sex and relationships.

Prior sexual abuse can significantly impact a person's sexual development and behavior, mainly if the abuse occurred during childhood or adolescence. According to research, individuals who have experienced sexual abuse are at a greater risk of engaging in sexually inappropriate behavior later in life and experiencing other adverse outcomes such as depression, anxiety, and PTSD (Maniglio, 2009).

One potential explanation is that sexual abuse can disrupt normal sexual development, leading to confusion, shame, and other negative emotions around sexuality. This can manifest in a variety of ways, including engaging in sexually inappropriate behavior as a means of coping with the trauma of the abuse.

In addition, individuals who have experienced sexual abuse may struggle with guilt and self-blame, making it difficult to form healthy relationships and engage in healthy sexual behavior. This can lead to a greater risk of sexually inappropriate behavior and other sexual and interpersonal violence.

By providing appropriate support and intervention, parents can help their teenager overcome the effects of prior sexual abuse and develop healthy coping skills and attitudes towards sex and relationships. This can reduce the risk of sexually inappropriate behavior and other negative outcomes later in life.

Prior sexual victimization may impact a teen's sexual development and behavior and may increase the risk of engaging in sexually inappropriate behavior later in life. By recognizing the potential impact of prior sexual victimization and seeking appropriate support and resources, parents can help their teen overcome the effects of trauma and develop healthy coping skills and attitudes toward sex and relationships.

The Role of the Teen Perpetrator in Sexual Misconduct

Teenagers who have faced arrests for sexually inappropriate behavior and have also experienced prior sexual abuse must recognize that they are not alone in their journey. Numerous teenagers who have undergone similar circumstances grapple with emotions of shame, guilt, and confusion concerning their sexuality. By providing understanding and support, we can help these individuals navigate their experiences and find healing and strength amidst their challenges.

Teens need to know that if they are the victim of previous sexual, this was not their fault. However, now that they have acted out sexually, they must accept responsibility for their actions and the harm caused to others. With the proper support and intervention, anyone can overcome the effects of trauma and develop healthy coping skills and attitudes towards sex and relationships.

It's crucial to seek appropriate support and resources, such as therapy, counseling, and support groups, to help deal with the effects of prior sexual abuse and the consequences of your behavior. As parents, you can help find these resources and work with your teen to establish healthy boundaries around sex and relationships.

Remember that your teen can change their behavior and overcome the effects of prior sexual abuse. By seeking support and taking responsibility for the actions, your teen can develop healthy coping skills and attitudes toward sex and relationships that will serve him well throughout his life.

Here are some steps that a teenager who has been arrested for sexually inappropriate behavior and is also experiencing emotional pain from prior sexual abuse can consider taking:

Seek Support
Reach out to trusted friends, family members, or counselors to talk about your experiences and emotions. Having a support system can be crucial during challenging times.

Seek Professional Help
Consider seeking therapy or counseling from a mental health professional specializing in trauma and sexual abuse. They can provide guidance and support in processing emotions and developing coping strategies. One form of therapy that is effective for survivors of sexual abuse is trauma-focused cognitive-behavioral therapy (TF-CBT). TF-CBT is an evidence-based therapy that helps survivors of sexual abuse overcome trauma and develop healthy coping skills. It typically involves cognitive-behavioral techniques, such as exposure therapy and cognitive restructuring, and trauma-focused interventions, such as relaxation techniques and psychoeducation.

Practice Self-Compassion
Understand that healing takes time, and it's okay to have complex emotions. Be kind to yourself and avoid self-blame for past actions.

Educate Yourself
Learn about the impact of trauma and sexual abuse to better understand your emotions and reactions. Knowledge can empower you to navigate through your experiences more effectively.

Join Support Groups
Consider joining support groups or workshops for individuals who have experienced similar situations. Connecting with others who have gone through similar challenges can be comforting and beneficial.

Reach Out for Legal Advice
If you face legal consequences, consult an attorney specializing in juvenile law to understand your rights and options.

Engage in Healthy Activities
Focus on engaging in activities that promote positive well-being, such as exercise, hobbies, or creative outlets.

Communicate with Authorities
If you haven't already, ensure open and honest communication with legal professionals involved in your case.

Remember, seeking help and support is a sign of strength, and taking steps toward healing and personal growth can lead to a brighter future. Teach your teen to establish healthy boundaries around sex and relationships. By providing this support and intervention, parents can help their teen develop healthy coping skills and attitudes towards sex and relationships.

Teenagers need to understand that engaging in sexually inappropriate behavior does not reflect their worth as a person. Separating the behavior from the person and working toward changing the behavior while also focusing on building healthy relationships and developing healthy coping skills.

Finally, teenagers need to understand that recovery from sexual abuse is a process and that it may take time and effort to overcome the effects of trauma. However, with the proper support and resources, it is possible to build a healthy future and to move beyond the pain of the past.

| 8 |

Safety Planning and Oversight

When a teenager is accused of sexually inappropriate behavior, it can be challenging and stressful for their parents. Creating a thorough, healthy living plan is one of the most essential measures parents can take to support their child's recovery and guarantee the safety of others.

A comprehensive healthy living strategy should encompass various situations and environments, including home, education, travel, and the community. Assessing each setting is crucial to identifying potential risks or factors contributing to inappropriate behavior. By proactively recognizing these dangers, individuals can implement measures to promote a safe and respectful environment in all aspects of their lives. Here are some essential factors to consider when developing a "Healthy Living Plan":

Informed Oversight
Supervision is essential during social events, including sleepovers, gatherings, and interactions with smaller children or vulnerable groups. Parents must remain vigilant and closely monitor their teens at all times to ensure that no harm is caused to anyone else. Maintaining constant supervision can help prevent inappropriate behavior and promote the safety and well-being of others.

Accountability and Conversation
Maintaining an open and honest conversation with your child and holding them accountable for their actions is paramount. This

involves having frequent conversations about how their behaviors impact others and the potential consequences. Additionally, parents may opt for implementing a system of responsibility, such as a behavior contract or daily check-ins, to monitor their child's progress and ensure adherence to the healthy living plan. By establishing such measures, parents can actively engage in their child's development and promote responsible behavior.

Using the Bathroom

Using the bathroom can be a high-risk situation for teens who have engaged in sexually inappropriate behaviors. Establishing explicit rules for restroom use in public locations, such as shops or restaurants, and at home is critical. Implementing door locks or monitoring during bathroom breaks can help ensure safety and prevent potentially harmful incidents. These actions will reduce the potential of future allegations of inappropriate sexual behaviors, and your teen will want to do anything possible to prevent future allegations. Proactively managing this aspect of their teen's behavior can significantly reduce risks and foster a secure environment for everyone involved.

Technology Use

Teenagers who have engaged in sexually inappropriate conduct may be at risk when using technology. It's critical to closely monitor your child's online and social media use and establish clear guidelines for acceptable behavior. Implementing parental control software or setting limits on websites and apps their children can access can be effective measures to protect them from potential dangers.

Peer Relationships

Peer relationships can significantly impact adolescent conduct, so keep an eye on your child's social contacts. Promoting good social interactions and providing opportunities for healthy social pursuits is critical. Limiting social activities or encounters with certain peers who may pose a danger to your teen or others may be considered by parents.

Therapy and Treatment

Working with competent experts who can help your child comprehend the severity of their behavior and work toward recovery is critical. Individual or family counseling, group therapy, and specialty therapeutic programs may be included. Parents may also seek help from peer support organizations or other parents who have experienced similar situations.

School and Society

Parents should consider including their child's school and community in their plan for healthy living. This can include carefully communicating with school officials or teachers. Be mindful of limiting only information needed to support and protect your teen. Too much information can backfire and cause severe repercussions for you and your teen. When this is done appropriately, the school officials will see your support and accountability for your teen to find a successful academic outcome. It's also critical to speak with neighbors or community members affected by your child's conduct and set ground rules for encounters with them.

Creating a healthy living plan (Safety Plan) can be a time-consuming and ongoing process. Still, it is necessary to ensure the safety of others and to aid in your teen's recovery.

Here are some additional measures parents can follow to create a healthy lifestyle plan:

- Ask for help from skilled professionals, like clinicians or therapists, who can help you plan a healthy lifestyle that covers everything.
- Look for possible dangers or sources of stress in different places, like at home, school, on the way to work, or in the community, and devise ways to deal with them.
- Set clear rules and expectations for your teens' behavior, such as how to use the bathroom or act in social situations.
- Put educated oversight and responsibility first and foremost.

When creating a Healthy Living Plan for adolescents, parents should consider potential risk factors, including substance use, mental health issues, and exposure to stress. Identifying any underlying problems that may contribute to inappropriate behavior and addressing them is crucial.

Providing your teen with appropriate therapy and support is essential to help them navigate challenges and promote positive growth. By recognizing and addressing these factors, parents can develop a comprehensive plan that effectively supports your teen's well-being and development.

Additionally, parents should take note of and confirm any of the following changes in their child's behavior:

- Secretive conduct, particularly near technological devices.
- Preoccupation with erotic subjects or imagery.
- Sexualized words or conduct with smaller children or creatures.
- Isolation from others or trouble sustaining good connections.
- Mood fluctuations or abrupt behavioral shifts.
- Abuse of substances or other self-destructive habits.
- Angry or hostile feelings toward others.
- Difficulties with sensitivity or comprehending the emotions of others.
- Issues with impulse control or decision-making.
- Denial or reduction of their actions or the damage they have caused.

It's important to note that not all teenagers who participate in sexually inappropriate behavior will display these behaviors, and not all teens who display these behaviors have engaged in such conduct. However, these behaviors, ideas, and actions can be red flags for parents to be watchful and seek assistance if necessary.

However, these behaviors, ideas, and actions can be red flags for parents to be watchful and seek assistance.

Recognizing Abnormal Sexual Behavior in Adolescents
Identifying inappropriate or abusive sexual behavior in teens is crucial. Several signs can raise concern:

Displaying Sexual Knowledge Beyond Their Age
If your child exhibits sexual knowledge or behavior beyond what's expected for their age group, it might indicate they've been exposed to explicit sexual content through abuse or media.

Secretive Behavior
If your child becomes secretive about their online activities or friendships, having a respectful conversation about their privacy and safety is advisable.

Sexual Interest in Younger Children
An older child showing a sexual interest in much younger children is a red flag that needs to be addressed with professional help.

Use of Force or Manipulation
A child using force, threats, or manipulation to engage in sexual activity with others is a serious concern requiring immediate professional intervention.

Compulsive Sexual Behavior
Obsessive interest in sexual activities, compulsive masturbation that doesn't respond to limits, or the inability to control sexual impulses indicate potential sexual behavior problems.

Not all children and adolescents with sexual behavior issues have been victims of sexual abuse. In outpatient treatment programs, as many as half of the teenagers have not been sexually abused. However, other factors can contribute to developing inappropriate sexual behavior, such as Attention Deficit Hyperactivity Disorder (ADHD), substance abuse, poor social skills, early exposure to sexually explicit material, social alienation, and unstable home environments.

Sample Healthy Living Plan

This Healthy Living Plan aims to provide a structured framework for the teen to stay on track with their treatment and avoid further inappropriate behaviors. It emphasizes the importance of developing healthy coping mechanisms, seeking support, and being accountable for their actions. By following this plan, the teenager can work towards healing and making positive changes in their life.

- Attend all required therapy sessions and follow the treatment plan the therapist sets.
- Avoid all contact with the victim and their family members.
- Abstain from using drugs or alcohol.
- Refrain from accessing or viewing any sexually explicit material, including pornography.
- Limit social media use and only communicate with friends and family members who are supportive and understanding.
- Report any feelings of temptation or urges to act out inappropriately to the therapist or parent immediately.
- Develop healthy coping mechanisms for stress or difficult emotions, such as exercise, meditation, or journaling.
- When feeling overwhelmed or tempted, seek support from trusted friends, family members, or mentors.
- Work with the therapist and parent to develop a plan for returning to school or other social activities, if necessary.
- Regularly check in with the therapist and parent to discuss progress and new challenges or concerns.

It's important to note that the Healthy Living Plan should be reviewed and updated as the teenager progresses in their treatment and as new challenges arise. The plan should also be shared with responsible adults, such as teachers or coaches, who may be involved in the teenager's life to ensure consistent supervision and support.

In addition to the Healthy Living Plan, the teen and their parent or caregiver need to work on building a supportive and healthy environment at home and in the community. This can include identifying and addressing any underlying issues that may have contributed to the inappropriate behaviors, such as trauma, family conflict, or substance abuse.

Overall, the Healthy Living Plan is essential for promoting healing, accountability, and safety for teenagers and those around them. By working together and seeking support from trusted professionals and community members, the teenager and their family can move towards a brighter and healthier future.

A critical component of the Healthy Living Plan is informed supervision around younger children or those who may be vulnerable. This means that the teen should always be supervised around younger children and should not be left alone, even for short periods. This can be achieved by having another trusted adult present or using video or audio monitoring tools.

Another concern that should be addressed in the Healthy Living Plan is bathroom use. Teenagers should always use bathrooms in public places that are designated for their gender, and they should never be allowed to use a bathroom that is designated for the opposite gender. At home, the teenager should always use a bathroom that has a lock and should never share a bathroom with a younger sibling or another child.

The Healthy Living Plan should also outline who is responsible for accountability for the supervision and safety of the teen. This can include the parent or caregiver, a trusted family member or friend, or a professional, such as a therapist or probation officer. The plan should also outline the consequences for any plan violations, such as additional restrictions or increased supervision.

It's crucial to involve the teen in developing and implementing the Healthy Living Plan to ensure they understand the expectations and are invested in the process. The plan should be reviewed regularly with the teenager, and any changes or updates should be made as needed.

It's important to remember that the Healthy Living Plan is not meant to be punitive or restrictive but rather a tool to promote safety and accountability for the teen and those around them. By working together and seeking support from trusted professionals and community members, the teenager and their family can move towards a brighter and healthier future.

In addition to the above, the Healthy Living Plan should address other concerns specific to the teenager and their situation. This may include avoiding specific triggers or situations leading to inappropriate behavior, setting boundaries for social media and internet use, and identifying safe and appropriate teen activities.

The plan should also outline steps for the teen if they feel they are at risk of acting out sexually inappropriately. This may include reaching out to a trusted adult or professional for support, engaging in healthy coping mechanisms, and avoiding situations that may trigger inappropriate behavior.

It's important to note that the Healthy Living Plan may need to be adjusted over time as the teen progresses in their treatment and their situation changes. The plan should always be flexible and responsive to the teenager's needs and reviewed regularly to ensure it is still effective.

It's also vital for parents and caregivers to seek support for themselves during this process. This may include therapy, support groups, or contacting trusted family and friends. Taking care of one's emotional well-being can help parents and caregivers better support their teen and navigate the challenges of the situation.

The Healthy Living Plan is critical to helping a teenager who has acted out sexually inappropriately move toward a healthier and brighter future. Parents and caregivers can help promote safety, accountability, and healing by working with professionals, community members, and the teen.

In addition to developing the plan, it's essential to communicate clearly and openly with the teenager about the expectations and guidelines that are in place. This may involve having difficult conversations about the consequences of their actions and the steps that need to be taken to promote healing and prevent future harm.

As part of the Healthy Living Plan, it may also be helpful to identify and address any underlying issues or traumas contributing to the teenager's behavior. This may involve working with a therapist or other mental health professional to explore the root causes of the behavior and develop strategies for addressing them.

Ultimately, the Healthy Living Plan aims to promote safety, accountability, and healing for the teen while supporting their growth and development as they navigate the challenges of adolescence and young adulthood. With the proper support, guidance, and resources in place, teenagers who have acted out sexually inappropriately can move forward toward a brighter and healthier future.

Developing healthy relationships is an important part of adolescence and young adulthood. However, for teenagers who have acted out sexually inappropriately, it may be wise to take extra precautions and establish clear guidelines regarding dating and personal relationships.

As part of the Healthy Living Plan, it may be helpful to establish guidelines around dating and relationships that are tailored to the teenager's individual needs and circumstances. This may include:

Setting boundaries
Establishing clear boundaries around physical touch, communication, and other aspects of the relationship can help prevent inappropriate behavior. The teenager and their parents/caregivers should discuss and agree upon these boundaries and communicate them clearly to potential partners.

Accountability
The teen needs to understand that their actions have consequences and that they are responsible for their behavior. Establishing accountability measures, such as regular check-ins with a therapist or mentor, can help to promote responsible behavior and prevent relapse.

Honesty and openness
The teen should be encouraged to be open and honest with their partner about their past behaviors and the steps they are taking to address them. This can help to build trust and establish a foundation of healthy communication in the relationship.

Respect
The teen should be encouraged to treat their partner respectfully and seek out partners who share these values. This may involve discussing healthy relationship dynamics and identifying warning signs of abusive or unhealthy relationships.

Parental involvement
Depending on the teenager's age and level of independence, it may be appropriate for parents/caregivers to be involved in their dating life to some degree. This may involve meeting potential partners, establishing curfews, or limiting alone time.

| 9 |

Treatment Programs and Their Approach

Most treatment programs focus on personal responsibility, emphasizing honesty, responsibility, sensitivity, and integrity. They aim to help the adolescent understand that their behavior is a personal choice and that they must take responsibility for their actions.

The first step in treatment is to recognize and accept that the behavior is harmful. Therapists guide the adolescent toward understanding the harm their actions may have caused others. This empathetic approach forms the basis for change.

Skills such as impulse control, problem-solving, empathy, and social interaction are nurtured. The program also enhances protective factors like supportive relationships, academic achievement, and constructive hobbies. Furthermore, family therapy is integral to the treatment, helping parents and siblings understand and effectively deal with the situation.

Remember, early intervention can significantly improve the prognosis. Don't hesitate to seek help if you suspect your child exhibits inappropriate or harmful sexual behavior. With the proper support and therapy, your child can learn healthier ways to navigate their sexuality and relationships.

Treatment Expectations and Evaluating Progress for Adolescents with Sexual Behavior Problems

The treatment plan driving your child's treatment should guide an adolescent with sexual behavior problems toward a healthier, more respectful understanding of sexuality and interpersonal relationships. The whole person should be addressed. Low self-confidence can increase social isolation and loneliness and become a factor in acting out sexually. Many other significant personal characteristics should be addressed in the treatment. It's essential to note that progress may vary between individuals, and continuous evaluation is necessary to ensure effective treatment.

Navigating Treatment: Understanding Expectations for Adolescents Facing Sexual Misconduct

The Association for the Treatment and Prevention of Sexual Abuse (ATSA) established standards for treating youth who have engaged in sexually inappropriate behavior. Some of the key expectations include:

Comprehensive Assessment
Treatment should begin with a thorough assessment of the youth's needs, risk factors, and strengths, as well as their specific offending behaviors and any underlying issues that may have contributed to their behavior.

Individualized Treatment Plans
Treatment should be tailored to each youth's unique needs and circumstances, with specific goals and strategies for addressing their problematic behaviors and reducing their risk of reoffending.

Evidence-based Interventions
Treatment should be based on interventions that are effective in reducing sexual reoffending and improving overall functioning, such as cognitive-behavioral therapy, trauma-focused therapy, and social skills training.

Collaborative approach
Treatment should involve collaboration between the youth, their parents or caregivers, and the treatment providers, building positive relationships and encouraging open communication.

Ongoing evaluation
Treatment should be regularly evaluated to determine its effectiveness and make any necessary adjustments. It should continue until the youth has completed their treatment goals is demonstrates mastery of their behaviors and communication.

Overall, the goal of treatment for youth who have sexually inappropriately acted out is to help them develop healthy behaviors and relationships while reducing their risk of causing harm to others.

The ATSA standards suggest a youth entering treatment for sexually inappropriate behaviors should expect the following as part of the overall treatment:

Assessment	Assessment is the first step in developing an appropriate treatment plan. It involves gathering information about the youth's history, sexual behaviors, and other relevant factors contributing to their behavior. The assessment process may include interviews, questionnaires, and psychological testing. **Expectation for parents** Parents can expect to be involved in the assessment process and may need to provide information about their teen's history and behavior. **Expectations for teens** Teens can expect to be asked questions about their behavior, feelings, and thoughts related to their behavior.

Safety Planning	Safety planning involves identifying potential risks and developing strategies to manage those risks. This may involve creating a safety plan for the teen and their family or community, identifying potential triggers for their behavior, and establishing clear boundaries and rules around appropriate behavior.
Psychoeducation	Psychoeducation involves providing information and education about sexual behavior, sexual development, healthy relationships, and appropriate sexual boundaries. **Expectation for parents** Parents can expect to be involved in their teen's education about sexual behavior and healthy relationships. **Expectations for teen** Teens can expect to learn about healthy sexual development and appropriate sexual boundaries.
Cognitive Behavioral Therapy (CBT):	CBT involves identifying and changing negative thought patterns and behaviors. This may include addressing distorted thinking, developing problem-solving skills, and practicing new behaviors. **Expectation for parents** Parents can expect to be involved in the CBT process and may need to reinforce new behaviors at home. **Expectation for teen** Teens can expect to learn new coping skills and behaviors to replace negative ones.

Trauma-Informed Care	Trauma-informed care involves recognizing and addressing the impact of past trauma on a youth's current behavior. This may involve addressing issues related to abuse or neglect and providing support and guidance to help the teen heal from past trauma. **Expectation for parents** Parents can expect to work with the treatment provider to address any past trauma their teen has experienced and support their teen. **Expectations for teen** Teens can expect to receive support and guidance to help them heal from past trauma.
Family Involvement	Family involvement is an important component of treatment, as it can help support the teen's progress and reinforce new behaviors. Family involvement may include family therapy, education and training for parents, and support for siblings and other family members. **Expectation for parents** Parents can expect to be involved in their teen's treatment and may need to participate in family therapy or educational programs. **Expectations for teen** Teens can expect their family to be involved in their treatment and to provide support and reinforcement for new behaviors.

Collaboration	Collaboration between the treatment provider, the family, and other professionals involved in the teen's care is important to ensure everyone works together to support the teen's progress. **Expectation for parents** Parents can expect to work closely with the treatment provider and other professionals involved in their teen's care. **Expectations for teen** Teens can expect the treatment provider and other professionals involved in their care to work collaboratively to support their progress.
Cultural Competence	Cultural competence involves recognizing and respecting the cultural and ethnic background of the teen and their family and incorporating this knowledge into treatment. **Expectation for parents** Parents can expect the treatment provider to recognize and respect their family's cultural background. **Expectations for teen** Teens can expect the treatment provider to recognize their own cultural needs and expectations.

Overall, the standards for treating youth who have sexually inappropriately acted out are designed to provide a comprehensive, evidence-based approach to addressing the underlying issues contributing to the youth's behavior and promoting their healthy development and reintegration into the community. The involvement of family and collaboration between treatment providers and other professionals is critical to treatment success, as is the ongoing evaluation of treatment outcomes.

Expectations for Teens in Treatment

- You will need to go to counseling or therapy. This is where you can talk to someone who can help you understand why you acted out and how to prevent it from happening again.

- You will need to be honest. Sometimes, talking about what led you to act out can be challenging, but it's important to tell the truth so your counselor can help you.

- You will need to take responsibility for your actions. This means admitting what you did and how it affected others. It also means doing what you can to make things right.

- You will need to learn new ways to cope. Acting sexually inappropriately is not a healthy way to deal with problems. Your counselor can help you learn new, healthy ways to deal with stress or difficult situations.

- You will need to stay away from things that could trigger your behavior. This means avoiding pornography and situations where you might be tempted to act out. Remember, the goal of treatment is to help you get better and prevent this from happening again. It may be challenging, but you can improve if you are honest and work hard.

- When you get help for sexually inappropriate behavior, you will work with a counselor or therapist who will help you understand why you acted inappropriately and teach you new ways to cope with your feelings. You will learn to communicate better, make good choices, and understand healthy relationships.

- You may be asked to participate in group therapy with other teens who have acted inappropriately. You will learn to work

- together as a team to talk about what you're going through, share your feelings, and support each other.

- Your therapist will also talk with your parents about ways to support you at home and make sure you're safe. This may include rules to keep you and others safe and supervision around younger children.

Five-Step Treatment Plan for a Youth with Inappropriate Sexual Behavior

Step 1: Comprehensive Assessment

Conduct a thorough evaluation of the teenager's mental health, emotions, and behavior to identify underlying factors contributing to the inappropriate sexual behavior. Identify any history of trauma, abuse, or neglect that may be linked to their actions. Assess the level of risk for future incidents to determine appropriate supervision and treatment intensity.

Step 2: Goal Setting

Establish clear and achievable goals for the treatment plan. These may include:
- Reduce the frequency and intensity of sexually inappropriate behaviors.
- Develop healthy coping strategies to manage emotional distress and triggers effectively.
- Enhance awareness of healthy relationships and establish clear boundaries.
- Improve communication and problem-solving skills.
- Foster empathy and understanding of the consequences of their actions on others.

Step 3: Interventions

Implement a combination of evidence-based interventions:

- Individual psychotherapy to address underlying emotional issues and develop effective coping mechanisms.
- Family therapy to enhance communication and address family dynamics.
- Group therapy sessions to cultivate healthy relationships and practice communication and problem-solving skills.
- Behavioral interventions, such as contingency management, reinforce and discourage negative behaviors.
- Provide education on healthy sexual development, emphasizing the significance of boundaries and consent.
- Consider referrals to specialized services, such as trauma-focused therapy or substance abuse treatment, if needed.

Step 4: Measurement and Monitoring

Regularly assess the teenager's progress toward treatment goals and adjust the plan as necessary. Monitor their behavior and risk level for potential future incidents. Maintain open communication with the teenager and their family/caregivers to ensure the effectiveness and relevance of the treatment plan.

Step 5: Support and Follow-Up

Provide ongoing support and encouragement to the teenager and their family/caregivers throughout the treatment process. Offer resources and tools to reinforce the skills learned during therapy, schedule follow-up sessions to assess progress sustainability, and address any emerging challenges.

Remember, addressing inappropriate sexual behavior is a complex and challenging process that requires commitment and active involvement from the teenager and their family/caregivers. Following this five-step plan, we aim to foster a positive and supportive environment for the teenager to overcome these issues and develop healthier behaviors and relationships.

Treatment Duration for Teens with Sexual Behavior Problems

The duration of treatment for adolescents with sexual behavior problems largely depends on factors such as the duration of the problem, the teen's motivation to change, and the support they receive. Compulsive behaviors also contribute to the treatment duration. Generally, a treatment period of up to 18 months in a weekly outpatient program is common, with six months often considered the absolute minimum based on the needs of various teens presenting problems.

Treatment Progress Observation

A teen's progress in treatment for sexual behavior problems is evaluated based on specific, measurable goals and objectives. Successful treatment is reflected in the adolescent's cooperation, taking responsibility for their actions, altering harmful thought patterns, and demonstrating behavioral changes over time.

The Youth Needs and Progress Scale (YNPS) was published by the Department of Justice by Robert Prentky. The full article can be found at the ojp.gov and search for YNPS. See Appendix D.

Below are some indicators of treatment progress:

- **Acceptance of Responsibility: The adolescent acknowledges their inappropriate or illegal sexual behavior without denial.**

- **Progress Toward Treatment Goals: The teen actively works toward treatment objectives, demonstrating this through behavior.**

- Identifying Contributing Factors: The teen understands the elements that led to their abusive patterns.

- Making Positive Changes: The teen is actively resolving or changing the factors contributing to their abusive behavior.

- Empathy Towards Victims: The teen understands and empathizes with the harm inflicted on the victims of their actions.

- Handling Emotional Stress: The adolescent learns to manage emotional stress in non-harmful ways, changing negative feelings.

- Improved Self-Esteem: The teen starts to feel better about themselves.

- Healthy Sexual Fantasies: The teen begins to report fantasies involving responsible and consensual sexuality with same-age partners.

- Positive Social Activities: The teen engages in non-sexual social activities with other teens who are positive role models.

- Healthy Family Relationships: The teen fosters good relationships and interactions with family members.

- Openness and Honesty: The teen is transparent about their thoughts, fantasies, and behaviors.

- Control Over Sexual Arousal: Teens reduce and control their sexual arousal towards potential victims and in social or family situations.

- Fewer Harmful Fantasies: The teen has fewer fantasies involving victims and non-consenting sex and more fantasies involving healthy, consensual relationships.

- Rational Thinking: Teens can understand and counteract their irrational or distorted thinking.

- **Identifying Abusive Patterns:** The teen can recognize their abusive behavior patterns and seek help when these patterns re-emerge.

- **Assertiveness:** The adolescent can express their feelings and thoughts assertively.

- **Emotional Work:** The teen has addressed and worked through past trauma, including being a victim of abuse or experiencing significant loss.

- **Enjoyment in Normal Activities:** The adolescent can find pleasure in regular activities.

- **Transfer of New Behavior Patterns:** The teen can understand, communicate, and apply the new behavior patterns learned in treatment to their home and community life.

- **Family Involvement:** The adolescent has assisted family members in recognizing risk factors and behavioral patterns of re-offending. They also learn to manage these factors differently or seek help when needed.

| 10 |

Protecting Your Teen in the Online World

The digital age has brought unprecedented access to information and social connectivity. However, this open door to the world also exposes your teen to various risks, especially if they have previously engaged in inappropriate sexual behavior. This chapter aims to be a comprehensive guide for parents, offering actionable steps to safeguard your teen's online activities.

Smartphones: More Than Just a Phone

Action Steps:
1. **Lock Screen Security**: Use biometrics and a strong password for added security.
2. **App Approval**: Be the gatekeeper for app installations.
3. **Monitoring Software**: Install reputable monitoring software.
4. **Location Tracking**: Use built-in or third-party apps to know your teen's whereabouts.
5. **Regular Check-ins**: Periodically review your teen's phone with them present.

Smartphones are powerful tools that can either aid or hinder your teen's progress in treatment. A secure lock screen is your first line of defense against unauthorized use. Biometrics and strong passwords are a must. You should also be the one to approve any new apps; this ensures that only age-appropriate and safe apps are installed.

Monitoring software can help you keep an eye on text messages, calls, and app usage.

It's not about invasion of privacy; it's about ensuring their safety. Location tracking can also be beneficial for knowing where your teen is at all times. Regular check-ins, where you sit down and go through their phone together, can also be a healthy way to monitor activity without being overly intrusive.

Internet and Tablets: The Virtual Playground

Action Steps:
1. **Safe Browsing**: Enable safe search settings.
2. **Time Limits**: Use parental controls to set time restrictions.
3. **Content Filters**: Block inappropriate websites.
4. **VPN and Public Wi-Fi**: Educate them about the risks of public Wi-Fi and the benefits of VPNs.
5. **Check Browser History**: Periodically review the browser history.

The internet is a treasure trove of information, but not all that glitters is gold. Safe search settings can filter out most inappropriate content, but they're not foolproof. That's where time limits and content filters come in. Limit internet usage during unsupervised hours and block websites that are not conducive to their treatment. Public Wi-Fi networks are often less secure, making it easier for inappropriate content to slip through or compromise personal information. A VPN can provide an extra layer of security. Lastly, make it a habit to check the browser history. It's a straightforward way to see what your teen has been up to online.

Social Media: A Reality Check

Action Steps:
1. **Friend List**: Regularly review and approve new connections.
2. **Privacy Settings**: Maximize account privacy.
3. **Open Dialogue**: Discuss the dangers of oversharing.

4. **Social Media Breaks**: Encourage periods of social media detox.
5. **Check Direct Messages**: With consent, periodically review messages.

Social media platforms are a hotbed for potential issues, from cyberbullying to contact with strangers. Review your teen's friend list regularly and remove or block unfamiliar or suspicious profiles. Ensure their accounts are set to the highest privacy settings to minimize exposure. Open dialogue is crucial; your teen must understand the risks of sharing personal or explicit content. Encourage social media breaks to help them focus on real-world interactions. With your teen's consent, periodically reviewing direct messages may also be beneficial to ensure they are not engaging in risky behavior.

Navigating the digital world with a teen who has acted out inappropriately in a sexual manner is challenging but crucial. Your active involvement in their online activities is not about control but protection and guidance. By implementing these steps, you're setting your teen on a path to becoming a responsible digital citizen while ensuring their safety and compliance with their treatment program.

| 11 |

Navigating Dating and Personal Relationships

It's important to understand that engaging in healthy and safe relationships is essential to healthy living. Parents need to let their adolescents know they are supported in developing positive relationships and learning healthy ways to express themselves sexually. Here are some guidelines to help teens make healthy choices:

Be honest
It's essential to be honest with your partner about your past and present behaviors and any concerns or struggles with sexual behavior. Honesty and communication are key to building trust and a healthy relationship.

Practice safe sex
Always use protection and practice safe sex to prevent the spread of sexually transmitted infections and unplanned pregnancies.

Respect Boundaries
Respect your partner's boundaries and communicate your own. Don't pressure your partner into sexual activities they're not comfortable with.

Seek Support
If you're struggling with your sexual behaviors or feel like you may have a problem, seek support from a therapist, counselor, or support group.

Have a Safety Plan
If you're in a relationship with a risk of inappropriate sexual behavior, have a safety plan to prevent harm to yourself or others. This may include avoiding certain situations or locations or having a trusted friend or family member check in on you regularly.

Healthy relationships are built on mutual respect, trust, and open communication. By practicing safe and healthy sexual behaviors, you can enjoy fulfilling and satisfying relationships while protecting yourself and your partners.

Consider your partner's age
It's essential to be aware of the legal age of consent in your state or country and to ensure that any sexual activity is consensual and legal. If you're uncertain about your partner's age, ask for identification or avoid sexual activity until you are sure.

Be aware of power dynamics
If you're in a relationship with someone with more power or authority than you, such as a teacher, coach, or boss, be aware of the potential for exploitation or abuse. Make sure that any sexual activity is consensual and that you're comfortable with the dynamics of the relationship.

Know your rights
You can say no to any sexual activity at any time, even if you've had sexual activity with your partner before. You also have the right to report inappropriate or illegal behavior to the authorities.

Responsibilities for Accountability and Supervision
As part of your Healthy Living plan, we want to ensure that you're accountable for your actions and that appropriate supervision is in place to ensure your safety and the safety of others. Here are some guidelines for accountability and supervision:

You are responsible for your actions
You are responsible for any actions you take and for following the guidelines of your Healthy Living plan. If you violate any of these guidelines, you may face consequences.

Trusted adult supervision
We recommend that a trusted adult supervise you when there may be a risk of inappropriate sexual behavior, such as around younger children or in public restrooms. This adult should know your situation and understand the importance of supervision.

Accountability check-ins
It would help if you had regular check-ins with a trusted adult, such as a parent or therapist, to discuss any concerns or struggles with your behaviors. These check-ins can help you stay accountable and on track with your Healthy Living plan.

By following these guidelines for dating and personal relationships, taking responsibility for your actions, and having appropriate supervision, you can continue developing healthy and safe relationships while maintaining accountability and safety.

Tailoring these recommendations to the teenager's age, maturity level, and specific circumstances is essential. It may be helpful to involve a therapist or counselor in creating a Healthy Living plan and discussing strategies for healthy dating and relationships.

| 12 |

Communicating After the News

Conversations With Your Teen About Their Sexual Behavior

Initiate open conversations with your teen about their treatment progress. Please encourage them to share what they're learning rather than prying into the specifics of their past behavior. Emphasize discussions about the consequences of their actions and how to make healthier choices.

Handling Denial of Inappropriate Behavior

It's normal for teens to initially deny the extent of their sexual behavior, especially when discussing with loved ones they fear disappointment. In time, with counseling and a supportive environment, most adolescents gradually disclose the full extent of their behaviors. It's crucial to listen to your teen and reassure them that changes in their story over time are acceptable. Supporting their denial, however, can hinder their process of coming to terms with their actions.

Discussing the Situation with School Personnel

Discussing your child's sexual behavior problems with select school personnel is appropriate if the behavior occurred at the school or the child's impulsiveness puts others at risk. A safety plan should be established and communicated if your teen has a history of sexual harassment or bullying at school.

Trusting Your Teen Around Younger Children

As a preventive measure against potential sexual misconduct, it's advised that your teen not be left alone with younger children for a long time. Although your teen might have good intentions, poor impulse control could lead to incidents. Close supervision and limiting access to younger children can reduce potential allegations and foster a safe environment. The consequences of one impulsive opportunity could lead to a lifetime of consequences.

Will My Child Grow Up to Become an Adult Sex Offender?

Limited long-term research exists on children and adolescents with sexual behavior problems, but available research suggests most youth do not continue the behaviors into adulthood. Many adolescents with sexual behavior problems transition into healthy and productive adult lives with minimal interruptions to their goals.

Supporting Your Child's Treatment Process

Engage with your teen's treatment by reviewing their workbooks or handouts, speaking with the therapist, and attending family therapy sessions. Remember, much of their work in treatment will be very sensitive to fear of embarrassment. Model appropriate boundaries and respect for your teen's journey. Your involvement is crucial to your teen's recovery.

Confronting the Uncomfortable: Mastering Difficult Conversations

When a teenager has been arrested for sexually inappropriate behaviors, it can be challenging to know who to tell and who to keep the information from. It is important to remember that while some level of confidentiality may be necessary, seeking appropriate support and resources to address the issue and prevent further harm is essential.

First and foremost, parents should prioritize the safety and well-being of their child and any victims involved. This may involve reporting the behavior to legal and mental health professionals and informing any necessary family members or caregivers who may need to be aware of the situation. It may also be necessary to inform the school if the behavior occurred on school grounds or involved classmates.

Regarding sharing the information with friends and extended family members, carefully consider who needs to know and why it is necessary. While it can be tempting to confide in close friends and family members for support, it is essential to respect the privacy and confidentiality of the situation and only share information on a need-to-know basis. Remember, the identity of the victim is never to be disclosed. This is vital to remember through all phases of treatment. The victim and their family have the right to talk about what happened. But, the teen and family who caused the harm can never identify the victim by name.

Parents may also consider seeking support groups or therapy to help them cope with the situation's emotional impact and to provide a safe space for open dialogue and support. Ultimately, the goal should be to work towards positive change and to prioritize the safety and well-being of all parties involved.

Additionally, parents should be aware of any legal requirements for reporting the behavior and any potential consequences or penalties for failing to report. Depending on the severity of the behavior and the child's age, there may be legal and ethical obligations to report to the appropriate authorities.

Ultimately, sharing the information with others should be based on the child's needs and the safety of any victims involved. Parents should prioritize seeking appropriate support and resources while respecting privacy and confidentiality. Remember, what is said will always be public in years to come.

If parents are unsure who to talk to or how to seek support, they may consider consulting with a legal or mental health professional specializing in these issues.

Additionally, various online and community-based resources are available for parents and families dealing with sexually inappropriate behaviors by their teens.

When Your Teenager's Actions Cross the Line

There's Hope After Being Arrested for Sexually Inappropriate Behaviors:

An Open Letter from Mom & Dad

Hey, buddy. We know that you're going through a tough time right now. Being arrested for sexually inappropriate behavior can be scary and confusing. You need to know you're not alone and that there is hope for a better future.

First, you need to understand that what you did was not okay. We love and support you, but we also want you to take responsibility for your actions and understand how your actions impacted others. We encourage you to work with your legal and mental health professionals to make things right and move forward.

You can learn from this experience and grow into a better person. You can make things right and work towards a positive future. It's okay to make mistakes, but to take responsibility for your actions and work toward a positive future is in your hands. We are here to support you every step of the way and believe in you. You can get through this, and we are here to help.

Remember, your past mistakes do not define you, but how you handle this and make changes for your future will identify who you are.

We love you, and we are here for you.

Take care, we love YOU!
Mom & Dad

> *Here's an example of a conversation between a parent/caregiver and their teenage son after being arrested for sexually inappropriate behavior.*

Sample Conversation: Parent & Teen

Parent: I want to talk with you about what happened and how we can move forward. First, I want you to know that I love you and am here to support you through this.

Teenage son: I'm sorry, Mom/Dad. I messed up.

Parent: I know this situation is difficult, but we must face it together. Can you tell me what happened and why it happened?

Teenage son: I don't know why I did it. I just felt like I couldn't control myself.

Parent: It's okay; we'll work on understanding why it happened to ensure it doesn't happen again. We must take responsibility for our actions and work towards making things right.

Teenage son: What's going to happen to me now?

Parent: We must work with legal and mental health professionals to develop rehabilitation and community reintegration plans. We must also prioritize healthy attitudes and behaviors towards sex and relationships.

Teenage son: What about the victim?

Parent: We must take responsibility for our actions and ensure the victim receives the support and resources they need. We'll work with professionals to make things right as much as possible.

Teenage son: What about the future? Will this affect me for the rest of my life?

Parent: It's possible, but we'll work on that when it comes up. Let's focus on what we control and what will help everyone the most. We must make positive changes and move towards a healthier and more positive future.

Sample Conversation: Parent & Family Member

Parent: I wanted to talk to you about something about our son. He's been arrested for sexually inappropriate behavior, and we're taking this very seriously.

Family member: Oh my goodness, I had no idea. Is he okay? What can we do to help?

Parent: Right now, we're focused on getting him the support and treatment he needs to understand why he did what he did and how to make sure it never happens again. But we also want to make sure that those in our family who may be at risk are aware of the situation and can take any necessary precautions.

Family member: Of course, we want to make sure everyone is safe. What can we do to support you and your son during this time?

Parent: Knowing that we have your love and support means a lot to us. We're working closely with mental health professionals and legal counsel to navigate this situation, but it can be a challenging and emotional process. We appreciate any support or understanding you can offer.

> *The parents are honest and transparent with their family members about their son's situation while prioritizing the safety of those at risk. The conversation emphasizes the importance of support and understanding from family members during a challenging time.*

Parent: We also want to make sure that we're doing everything we can to help our son understand the impact of his actions and how to move forward positively. It's a complicated situation, but we're committed to doing whatever it takes to keep everyone safe and to help our son get the support and treatment he needs.

Family member: That doesn't sound easy. Is there anything specific we can do to help?

Parent: Right now, we're focused on getting him the best possible treatment and support, but we may need some help. If we do, we'll let you know. In the meantime, knowing that we have your love and support means a lot to us.

Family member: Of course, we're here for you. Is there anything we should know about the situation to make sure we're taking the right precautions?

Parent: We're working closely with mental health professionals and legal counsel to ensure we do everything possible to protect those at risk. We don't want to share too much information, but we want to ensure everyone is aware of the situation and can take any necessary precautions.

> *In this example, the parent is open and honest with their family members about the situation while also protecting their son's privacy and confidentiality and the victim's privacy. The conversation emphasizes the importance of support and understanding from family members and the need to prioritize the safety of those who may be at risk.*

Parent: Thank you for understanding. It's been a tough time for all of us, but we're doing our best to get through it.

Family member: Absolutely, we'll be here for you no matter what. Is there anything else we should know about how we can help or support you during this time?

Parent: Right now, we're just taking things one day at a time and focusing on getting our son the support and treatment he needs. But if we need any help down the road, we'll definitely reach out to you. Just knowing that we have your love and support means a lot to us.

Family member: Of course, we're here for you. And please don't hesitate to let us know if there's anything we can do to help.

> *The parent is grateful for their family member's understanding and support during a difficult time. They emphasize the importance of taking things one day at a time, focusing on getting their son the help he needs and recognizing the value of having a supportive family network. The conversation reinforces the idea that open and honest communication is key to navigating a challenging situation like this one.*

Sample Conversation: Parent & Neighbor

Here's an example of a parent talking to a neighbor who has small children:

Parent: Hi, I wanted to talk to you about something important. My son has been arrested for sexually inappropriate behaviors, and I wanted to let you know out of concern for your own children's safety.

Neighbor: Oh my goodness, I had no idea. Thank you for telling me. What can I do to protect my children?

Parent: I think the most important thing is to be aware of the potential risk and to take appropriate precautions. I would encourage you to have a conversation with your children about safe and appropriate boundaries and to be mindful of any behavior that seems concerning or inappropriate.

Neighbor: That makes sense. Do you have any resources or advice on how to talk to my children about this?

Parent: Yes, there are a number of resources available for parents on how to talk to children about safe boundaries and sexual safety. I can provide you with some information and resources if that would be helpful.

Neighbor: That would be great, thank you. And please let me know if there is anything else I can do to help or support you and your son during this difficult time.

Parent: Thank you, I appreciate that. We're working with mental health professionals and support groups to address the behavior and prevent further harm. We need to have the support and understanding of our community as we work towards positive change.

Neighbor: I understand. It's important to get the right support and resources in place. I hope things get better for your family and your son.

Parent: Thank you. I appreciate your understanding and support. And please don't hesitate to reach out if you have any questions or concerns in the future.

> *The parent prioritizes the safety and well-being of the neighbor's children by being open and honest about their own son's behavior while also providing resources and support to help the neighbor protect their own children. The conversation emphasizes the importance of open communication and community support in addressing sexually inappropriate behaviors and preventing further harm.*

Parents model transparency about their child's behavior with those who may be at risk while respecting the victim's identity and your child's privacy and right to confidentiality. This can be a delicate balance, and parents may benefit from seeking guidance from mental health professionals or legal counsel on navigating these conversations.

In addition, parents need to be mindful of the impact that discussing their child's behavior may have on their emotional well-being. It can be challenging to navigate the complex emotions and reactions that come with confronting sexually inappropriate behaviors, and parents may need to prioritize their self-care and support as well.

Talking to others about your child's sexually inappropriate behaviors can be challenging and emotionally taxing. Still, it is essential in preventing further harm and protecting those at risk. By prioritizing the safety and well-being of all parties involved and seeking appropriate support and resources, parents can work towards positive change and help their children move forward.

Remember, as caregivers, you are not alone in this process. Support groups and resources are available for parents of teens who have acted out sexually, as well as for the victims and their families. These resources can provide guidance, support, and a sense of community for parents who may be feeling isolated or overwhelmed.

Additionally, parents must take care of themselves and prioritize their own emotional and mental health. This may involve seeking therapy or counseling, joining a support group, or finding other healthy outlets for stress and emotions.

Ultimately, the key to navigating these conversations is open communication, transparency, and a commitment to protecting the safety and well-being of all parties involved. With the proper support and resources, parents can help their teens move toward positive change and healing while protecting their community's safety.

Sample Conversation: Parent & School Faculty

Parent: Hi, I wanted to touch base with you about my son. He's been going through a really difficult time lately, and I wanted to let you know what's going on.

School Administrator: Of course, I'm here to listen. What's been happening?

Parent: My son has had some inappropriate behaviors recently. We're taking the situation very seriously, and he's getting the help he needs, but we wanted to make sure you were aware of the situation.

School Administrator: Thank you for letting me know. Is there anything specific you need from the school at this time?

Parent: Right now, we're working closely with the professionals to ensure we're doing everything we can. We don't want to share too much information, but we want to ensure everyone is aware of the situation and can take any necessary precautions. We hope to work together to create a safe and supportive environment for our son and everyone else in the school.

School Administrator: We're committed to ensuring our students feel safe and supported. We'll work with you to create a plan that addresses everyone's needs and ensures the safety of all students.

In this example, the parent is open and honest with the school administrator about their son's situation while also protecting their son's privacy and confidentiality. The conversation emphasizes the importance of working together to create a safe and supportive environment for all students while recognizing the need for confidentiality and privacy.

The conversation also highlights the importance of addressing the needs of all students and taking any necessary precautions to ensure their safety. The parents acknowledge that they are working closely with mental health professionals and legal counsel to address the situation, and the school administrator offers their support in creating a plan that meets everyone's needs.

Parents must have open and honest conversations with school administrators when their child is struggling. By working together, parents and school administrators can create a plan supporting the student while addressing the school community's needs. The conversation should prioritize confidentiality and privacy while emphasizing the importance of creating a safe and supportive environment for all students.

Parents must also understand their legal obligations in reporting their child's behavior to the school. Depending on the severity of the behavior and the potential risk to other students, parents may be legally required to disclose their child's situation to the school. Many parents seek legal guidance and understand their obligations to act in their child's best interests and the school community.

In addition to communicating with school administrators, parents may also need to communicate with other parents or community members. They are being honest and transparent about the situation while respecting the privacy and confidentiality of all involved. Parents may consider speaking with a trusted community leader, such as a religious leader or community organizer, to get guidance on how to best communicate with others and address any concerns or questions that may arise.

When Your Teenager's Actions Cross the Line

| 13 |

Final Thoughts

As we reach the end of this guide, it's important to reflect on the journey you've embarked upon as a parent or caregiver of a youth with sexual behavior problems. The issue of sexual behavior problems in teenagers is a complex and sensitive one, often fraught with shame, confusion, and fear. This book aims to provide you with the tools, knowledge, and resources to navigate this challenging period in your child's life. Remember, you're not alone, and help is available.

Key Takeaways

1. Understanding the Issue: Sexual behavior problems in teens are not just "phases" or "youthful indiscretions." They are serious issues that require immediate attention.

2. Open Communication: Establishing a line of open and honest communication with your teen is crucial. It's the first step in understanding what led to these behaviors and how to address them.

3. Professional Help: Therapists, counselors, and other professionals are trained to help families in situations like yours. Don't hesitate to seek their guidance.
4. Legal Consequences: Understand that these behaviors can have severe legal repercussions. It's essential to consult with legal professionals to know what you're up against.

5. **Family Involvement:** This is not just a "teen issue." It affects the entire family, and everyone's cooperation and involvement are vital for a successful outcome.

Moving Forward

The road ahead may be long and filled with challenges, but it's important to stay committed. Your teen can change, but it will require consistent effort from both you and them. Keep the lines of communication open, continue to educate yourself and your family, and don't lose hope. Many families have been in your shoes and have come out stronger on the other side.

Final Thoughts

As we close this chapter, remember that your love and support are the most powerful tools you have. Your teen has crossed a line, but that doesn't mean they can't find their way back. With the right help and a committed approach, it's possible to redirect their path and help them become responsible, empathetic adults. I have worked with thousands of teens and families who have walked in your shoes. I can say confidently that nearly all put the effort and commitment in, and it paid off.

Thank you for taking the time to educate yourself through this guide. The journey may be tough, but you're already taking the right steps by seeking knowledge and help. Good luck and take care, and always remember YOU matter!

Rick

Youtube: @Tools4TeensandParents
www.sayhelp.net
www.tools4teens.net

Appendix A

Parents with a history of prior sexual abuse

Kendall-Tackett, K. A. (2002). A trauma-informed approach to parenting sexually abused children. Journal of Child Sexual Abuse, 11(4), 43-63.

This article explores the impact of childhood sexual abuse on parenting and provides guidance for parents who have experienced sexual abuse and are now dealing with a child who has engaged in sexually inappropriate behavior. The author argues that parents who have experienced sexual abuse may struggle with feelings of shame, guilt, and blame, which can make it difficult for them to provide their child with the support and guidance they need.

The article recommends that parents who have experienced sexual abuse seek out counseling and support to help them address their own trauma and develop healthy coping mechanisms. It also emphasizes the importance of creating a safe and supportive environment for the child and working collaboratively with mental health professionals to develop a comprehensive treatment plan.

The article highlights the importance of a trauma-informed approach to parenting, which involves understanding the impact of trauma on both the parent and child and recognizing the potential for triggers and re-traumatization. It also stresses the importance of developing a solid support network, including family, friends, and mental health professionals, to help the parent navigate the challenges of parenting a sexually abused child.

Overall, the article underscores the complex and challenging nature of parenting a child who has engaged in sexually inappropriate behavior, particularly for parents who have experienced sexual abuse. However, it also provides hope and guidance for parents seeking to support their child through this challenging time, emphasizing the importance of self-care and seeking out support.

The article "Parenting a child who has sexually abused: perspectives of parents who experienced sexual abuse in childhood" by Proulx, Hébert, and Lavoie, published in the Journal of Child Sexual Abuse in 2018, discusses the challenges and difficulties faced by parents who have experienced sexual abuse in their childhood and are now parenting a child who has sexually abused another.

The study used a qualitative approach and involved interviews with nine parents who had experienced sexual abuse in their childhood and were currently parenting a child who had sexually abused. The findings of the study indicated that these parents faced numerous challenges and difficulties, including feelings of shame, guilt, and blame. They struggled with their own past experiences of abuse, which made it difficult for them to provide the necessary support and guidance to their child.

The study also found that these parents experienced a lack of support from the community, including family members, friends, and professionals. They felt isolated and stigmatized, which made it challenging for them to seek help and support.

Based on the study's findings, the authors recommend several action steps for parents parenting a child who has been sexually abused and has experienced sexual abuse in their childhood.

These action steps include:

Seeking support: Parents should seek support from professionals who are trained in working with families dealing with sexual abuse. They should also reach out to support groups and other organizations that can provide them with the necessary support and guidance.

Working through their own trauma: Parents need to work through their own trauma and seek therapy if necessary to address any unresolved issues related to their past experiences of abuse. This will help them to provide better support to their child.

Maintaining a balance: Parents must balance providing support to their child and setting appropriate boundaries. This can be challenging, but it is crucial to ensure the safety of all family members.

Educating themselves: Parents should educate themselves about sexual abuse and its impact on children. They should also educate themselves about the legal and ethical responsibilities that come with parenting a child who has sexually abused another child.

Fostering open communication: Parents should foster open communication with their child and create a safe environment where their child feels comfortable discussing their feelings and experiences.

The article emphasizes the importance of supporting parents who have experienced sexual abuse in their childhood and are parenting a child who has been sexually abused. The authors recommend action steps for parents to address their challenges and difficulties and better support their teen.

Appendix B

Glossary of Terms

Okay, I understand some of these terms are common, but I've had many questions over the years about some of these terms.

Abstinence	Abstinence is the decision to not engage in sexual activity.
Age of Consent	The age of consent is the legal age at which someone can give explicit, informed, and voluntary consent to engage in sexual activity. This age varies by state and country.
Child Molestation	Child Molestation involves sexual activity with a minor (a person under the age of consent). It's a severe crime with harsh legal penalties.
Child Pornography (CP)	Child pornography is any type of sexually explicit material that features minors. Possession or distribution of child pornography is illegal and can result in severe legal consequences.
Child Sexual Exploitation Material (CSEM)	Child Sexual Exploitation Material (CSEM) online refers to sexualized content depicting minors that is exploitative but does not fall within the classification of nationally illegal child sexual abuse material (CSAM). It can also include non-illegal images in a series with CSAM as exploitation material due to its investigative relevance and the context of exploitation in which it was generated. CP, CSEM, and CSAM are often used interchangeably.
Consent	Consent is the agreement to participate in sexual activity. It is essential to understand that individuals must give clear, informed, and voluntary consent before engaging in sexual activity.

Consequence	A consequence is a result or outcome that occurs because of a specific behavior or action. Consequences can be positive or negative, and it is crucial to understand the potential consequences of sexually inappropriate behavior.
Contraception	Contraception is the use of methods or devices to prevent pregnancy during sexual activity.
Emotional Consequences	Emotional consequences refer to the negative emotional impact that sexually inappropriate behavior can have on the individual and their family and friends. This can include shame, guilt, and other negative emotions.
Human Trafficking	Human Trafficking is the recruitment, transportation, transfer, harboring, or receipt of people through force, fraud, or deception, with the aim of exploiting them for profit. Men, women, and children of all ages and backgrounds can become victims of this crime in every region of the world. https://www.unodc.org/unodc/en/human-trafficking/human-trafficking.html
Indecent Exposure	This refers to the act of purposely displaying one's genitals (private parts) in public, causing others to feel uncomfortable or threatened.
Incest	This is sexual activity between family members or close relatives, which is illegal in many jurisdictions due to potential abuse and genetic issues.
Legal Consequences	Legal consequences refer to the legal punishments or penalties resulting from sexually inappropriate behavior. These can include fines, probation, or even imprisonment.
Lewd & Lascivious Behavior	Lewd and lascivious, also known as statutory rape, are actions of sexual nature that involve a person younger than 16 years. Given that people this age have not met the age of consent (varies by location), having any type of intimate contact with them is considered illegal, even if the relationship was consensual.

Masturbation	Masturbation is the act of stimulating one's genitals for sexual pleasure.
Menstruation	Menstruation is the monthly shedding of the uterus lining in females who have reached puberty. It is commonly referred to as a "period."
Non-Consensual Pornography	This refers to sharing or disseminating an individual's explicit images or videos without their consent, which can be a form of sexual cyber-harassment.
Ovaries	The ovaries are female reproductive organs that produce eggs and the female hormones estrogen and progesterone.
Penis	The penis is a male sexual organ used for urination and sexual activity. It contains erectile tissue that can become engorged with blood to produce an erection.
Puberty	Puberty is when a person's body changes from a child's to an adult's. It typically begins around age 8-13 for girls and 9-14 for boys.
Rape	Penetration, no matter how slight, of the vagina or anus with any body part or object, or oral penetration by a sex organ of another person, without the victim's consent. Attempts or assaults to commit rape are also included; however, statutory rape and incest are excluded.
Reproductive Health	Reproductive health refers to the physical, emotional, and social well-being related to the reproductive system and its functions.
Sexting	Includes using your phone, computer, or camera to take or send sexy messages or images — usually selfies. You might think that sexting is a harmless way to flirt or show your boyfriend or girlfriend that you're into them. But sexts can outlast your crush or even your relationship.

Sexual Abuse	Sexual abuse is any sexual activity that occurs without explicit, informed, and voluntary consent. This can include sexual assault but can also include any sexual behavior that is inappropriate or unwanted.
Sexual Assault	Sexual assault is any sexual activity that occurs without explicit, informed, and voluntary consent. This can include rape, sexual touching or groping, and other unwanted sexual activity.
Sexual Cyber-Harassment	Also known as "revenge porn," this involves sharing explicit photos or videos of someone without their consent, often with the intent to cause harm or distress. It's become available easily with cell phones' internet and social media access.
Sexual Exploitation	This involves taking non-consensual, unfair, or abusive sexual advantage of another for one's benefit. It can include creating or sharing explicit images without consent, voyeurism, or human trafficking.
Sexual Harassment	Sexual harassment is any unwanted or unwelcome sexual behavior or advances, including comments, touching, or other behaviors that create a hostile or uncomfortable environment.
Sexual Offender	A sex offender is someone who has been convicted of a sex crime, such as sexual assault or possession of child pornography.
Sexual Offender Registry	The sex offender registry is a public database of sex offenders. This database is intended to help law enforcement and the public keep track of sex offenders in their community.
Sexual Orientation	Sexual orientation refers to the gender(s) of the people an individual is attracted to. Common sexual orientations include heterosexual (attracted to people of the opposite gender),

		homosexual (attracted to people of the same gender), and bisexual (attracted to people of both genders).
	Stalking	While not always sexually motivated, stalking becomes sexual misconduct involving unwanted pursuit or attention with sexual intent.
	Testicles	The testicles are male reproductive organs that produce sperm and the male hormone testosterone.
	Vagina	The vagina is a female sexual organ used for sexual activity and childbirth. It is a muscular tube that connects the uterus to the outside of the body.

When Your Teenager's Actions Cross the Line

Appendix C

Article Summary: KNOW YOUR LABELS (FAQ) by SEIGFRIED-SPELLAR & ROGERS

The article "Know Your Labels" by SEIGFRIED-SPELLAR & ROGERS delves into the complexities of terms like "pedophiles," "child sex offenders," and "child pornography users." It aims to clarify misconceptions and provide a nuanced understanding of these terms.

The article also discusses the legal definitions, academic perspectives, and myths surrounding these topics. It emphasizes that not all pedophiles are child sex offenders and vice versa. The article also talks about the psychological aspects of child pornography users, including the reasons behind their collections and the types of content they may possess.

Key Points:

Terminology
- Pedophiles: A clinical term, not a legal one. Diagnostic criteria exist.
- Child Sex Offenders: Legal term, may or may not meet criteria for being a pedophile.
- Child Pornography Users: More numerous than contact child sex offenders.

Child Pornography (CP)
- Definition: Any visual depiction of sexually explicit conduct involving a minor.
- Types: Includes undeveloped film, digital images, etc.
- Terminology: Now referred to as "Child Sexual Exploitation Material" (CSEM).
- Arrests: Increase likely due to better law enforcement resources.

Child Pornography Collections
- Desensitization: Some users seek more extreme materials.

- Variety: Collections may include other forms of deviant pornography.
- Motivation: Not always due to sexual interest in children.

Pedophilia
- Diagnostic Criteria: Defined in the DSM 5.
- Prevalence: 3-5% in the male population; unknown in females.
- Alternative Label: Some use "Minor-Attracted Person" (MAP).

This summary aims to provide a clear and concise understanding of the article's key points, especially for teens and parents who may be involved in treatment or education on this topic.

Appendix D

Recommended Books

Safer Society Press - https://safersocietypress.org/store/

Healthy Families by Timothy Kahn
Current research indicates that parental involvement contributes to successfully treating children with sexual behavior problems. Timothy Kahn, author of Pathways, the best-selling adolescent treatment workbook, and Roadmaps to Recovery, a treatment workbook for children, has written Healthy Families to help parents effectively engage in their child's treatment. The book teaches parents to make positive, informed, healthy decisions as their children proceed through any outpatient or residential treatment program. Healthy Families includes an appendix with specific information for parents whose children are using Pathways or Roadmaps to Recovery in treatment; however, all parents with kids in treatment will benefit from the information in Healthy Families, and so will their children.

Pathways, 5th Edition by Timothy Kahn
The Pathways workbook has been a cornerstone in treating sexually aggressive youth since the first edition was issued twenty years ago. As the field has evolved and advanced, so has Pathways. This reflects current research and clinical experience with adolescents by focusing on strength-based methods to help clients develop healthy and productive lifestyles consistent with the Good Lives rehabilitation model.

Pathways continues to use a restorative justice theme emphasizing concern for restitution, development of victim empathy, and personal responsibility. The focus is shifted from the offense cycle to understanding the antecedents of a client's sexual acting out.

Stages of Accomplishment, 2nd Edition by Phil Rich
Stages of Accomplishment is a set of four interrelated workbooks that assist in treating sexually abusive or sexually troubled adolescents. Building from more straightforward ideas to more complex and richer concepts, the workbooks take youth through a series of guided exercises that touch on many of the most significant elements of treatment.

The Road to Freedom, 4th Edition by Jill S. Levenson, Ph.D. & John W. Morin, Ph.D.

The Road to Freedom has been a staple of adult offender treatment for two decades. In this new fourth edition, the authors have incorporated contemporary theories, models, and evidence-informed best practices for preventing sexual re-offending while keeping the structure of the previous edition to allow for an easy transition from old to new.

Framing sex offending within a larger context of relational patterns, The Road to Freedom helps each client learn to meet needs in healthy ways. A strengths-based focus on healthy sexuality and self-regulation avoids confrontational and shaming language.

What's Going on Down There?: A Boy's Guide to Growing Up – available on Amazon.com

Part manual, part older brother, this accessible guidebook from Karen Gravelle, the author of the perennial bestseller The Period Book, will empower adolescent boys with honest answers to all of their questions about what's really going on down there.

With 150,000 copies sold, this definitive illustrated guidebook to puberty--now updated with brand-new content relevant to today's kids--is the perfect companion for boys and parents seeking information about growing up and their changing bodies. The book addresses physical and emotional changes boys might expect, discusses what puberty is like for girls, and prepares readers to make intelligent choices about sex. Written in consultation with preteen boys, this guide offers a supportive, practical approach, providing clear and sensitive explanations of everyday experiences.

This revised edition features new sections on:
- body image and confidence
- sexual harassment and consent
- using social media safely

Appendix E

Summary: Youth Needs and Progress Scale Final Version

The measure is meant to guide long-term psychological health therapies, not re-offense risk. The project promotes resource allocation and juvenile triage by urgency. This is important since adolescents are developing rapidly and should not be managed like adults.

The Youth Needs and Progress Scale (YNPS) improves sexual offender treatment. The scale identifies interventions needed for tailored management and case strategies. The YNPS helps professionals plan cases and interventions by assessing behavior change over time.

The YNPS guides long-term psychological health therapy, not re-offense risk prediction. It improves communication between physicians and juvenile justice stakeholders. This helps handle juvenile sex offenders (this is the criminal justice term, not treatment providers) more effectively.

The scale prioritizes critical requirements to optimize results and save costs in juvenile management. The YNPS may enhance juvenile sex offender management, decrease jail costs, educate public policy and legislation, and improve results.

The final version includes a user guide and training materials and can be found on the National Center on the Sexual Behavior of Youth website under resources for downloading. As a parent or caregiver of a teen who has acted out in a sexually inappropriate way, ask your treatment provider to help you track your teen's progress throughout treatment with the YNPS.

The 22 items are scored on a 0-3 scale outlined below and can be used to reassess treatment needs and progress.

0 = No Intervention Need
1 = Possible/Limited Intervention Need
2 = Moderate Intervention

3 = Strong Intervention Need

Understanding Appropriate Sexual Behavior	Understanding the Consequences of Sexual Abuse	Sexual Thoughts - Frequency
Sexual Interests – Age and Consent	Sexual Attitudes and Beliefs	Sexual Behavior Management
Compassion for Others	Relationships with Peers	Emotion Management
Social Skills	Self-Confidence	School and Work Commitment
Use of Unstructured Time	Nonsexual Behavior Attitudes and Beliefs	Nonsexual Behavior Management
Client View of Primary Caregiver Relationship	Client View of Supportive Adult Relationships	Family Functioning
Living Situation - Safety and Stability	Involvement in Community Resources	Mental Health Management
Participation in Interventions		

Appendix F

References & Resources

American Academy of Child and Adolescent Psychiatry - Offers resources and information for parents and caregivers on a range of mental health and behavioral issues, including sexual behavior problems in children and adolescents: https://www.aacap.org/

American Academy of Pediatrics - Offers resources and support for pediatricians and families on a range of health issues affecting children and adolescents, including sexual health: https://www.aap.org/

American Association of Sexuality Educators, Counselors, and Therapists - Offers resources and support for professionals and families on promoting healthy sexuality and addressing sexual behavior problems: https://www.aasect.org/

American Bar Association. (2017). Restorative justice in the juvenile justice system. https://www.americanbar.org/groups/public_interest/child_law/resources/child_law_practiceonline/child_law_practice/vol-36/may-2017/restorative-justice/

American Civil Liberties Union. (n.d.). Juvenile sex offender registration. https://www.aclu.org/other/juvenile-sex-offender-registration

American Humane Association - Offers resources and support for families and professionals working with at-risk youth, including those who have experienced abuse or neglect: https://www.americanhumane.org/

American Psychological Association. (2015). Understanding and addressing juvenile sexual offending behavior.

https://www.apa.org/pi/families/resources/newsletter/2015/05/juvenile-sexual-misconduct

American Psychological Association. (2012). Juvenile sex offender treatment: A meta-analytic inquiry into the effectiveness of treatment for juveniles who have committed sexual offenses. https://www.apa.org/pubs/journals/releases/amp-67-4-285.pdf

American School Counselor Association - Offers resources and support for school counselors and families on a range of mental health and behavioral issues, including sexual behavior problems in children and adolescents: https://www.schoolcounselor.org/

American Association for Marriage and Family Therapy - Provides resources and support for families and professionals working with mental health and behavioral issues, including sexual behavior problems: https://www.aamft.org/

American Association of Sexuality Educators, Counselors, and Therapists (AASECT) - Offers resources and support for professionals and families on how to address sexual behavior problems in children and adolescents: https://www.aasect.org/

American Foundation for Suicide Prevention - Offers resources and support for individuals and families impacted by suicide and suicidal thoughts, which can be a risk factor for sexually inappropriate behavior: https://afsp.org/

Association for the Advancement of Evidence-Based Practice - Offers resources and support for professionals and organizations on how to incorporate evidence-based practices into their work with youth who have engaged in sexually inappropriate behavior: https://www.aaebp.org/

Association for Behavioral and Cognitive Therapies - Offers resources and support for professionals and families on evidence-based treatments for mental health and behavioral issues, including sexual behavior problems: https://www.abct.org/

Association for the Treatment and Prevention of Sexual Abuse (ATSA) - A professional organization focused on promoting evidence-based treatment for individuals who have engaged in sexually harmful behaviors. They offer resources for professionals and families on how to address sexual offending behavior: https://www.atsa.com/

Big Brothers Big Sisters of America - Offers mentorship programs and resources for youth, including those at risk of engaging in sexually inappropriate behavior: https://www.bbbs.org/

Boys and Girls Clubs of America - Offers after-school programs and resources for youth, including those at risk of engaging in sexually inappropriate behavior: https://www.bgca.org/

Boys Town - Offers resources and support for parents and caregivers on a range of parenting and family-related issues, including how to promote positive youth development and address concerning sexual behaviors in children and adolescents: https://www.boystown.org/

Campaign for Youth Justice - Advocates for ending the practice of trying youth as adults in the justice system, which can disproportionately impact youth of color and those with mental health and behavioral issues: https://www.campaignforyouthjustice.org/

Center for Sex Offender Management. (2008). Fact sheet: Juvenile sex offenders. https://www.csom.org/pubs/recidjuv.pdf

Centers for Disease Control and Prevention. (2019). Promoting positive youth development. https://www.cdc.gov/healthyyouth/protective/index.htm

Centers for Disease Control and Prevention - Offers resources and support for individuals and families impacted by a range of health issues, including sexual health: https://www.cdc.gov/

Childhelp - A non-profit organization that prevents child abuse and neglect through education, advocacy, and support services. They offer a hotline for parents and caregivers to get support and resources for addressing child abuse and neglect: https://www.childhelp.org/

Child Mind Institute - Offers resources and support for families and professionals on a range of mental health and behavioral issues affecting children and adolescents, including sexual behavior problems: https://childmind.org/

Child Welfare Information Gateway. (2016). Child sexual abuse: Definition, prevalence, and impact. U.S. Department of Health and Human Services, Children's Bureau. https://www.childwelfare.gov/pubPDFs/child-sexual-abuse.pdf

Darkness to Light - A non-profit organization that prevents child sexual abuse through education and training programs. They offer resources and training for parents, caregivers, and community members on how to recognize and prevent child sexual abuse: https://www.d2l.org/

International Association for the Treatment of Sexual Offenders - Offers resources and support for professionals working with individuals who have engaged in sexually inappropriate behavior: https://www.iatso.org/

International Society for the Prevention of Child Abuse and Neglect - Offers resources and support for individuals and organizations working to prevent child abuse and neglect, including sexual abuse: https://www.ispcan.org/

Mental Health America - Provides resources and support for individuals and families on a range of mental health issues, including trauma and recovery: https://www.mhanational.org/

National Alliance on Mental Illness - Offers resources and support for individuals and families impacted by mental illness, including those at risk of engaging in sexually inappropriate behavior: https://www.nami.org/

National Association for the Education of Young Children - Offers resources and support for parents and caregivers on promoting positive child development, including healthy sexuality and boundaries: https://www.naeyc.org/

National Association for Rational Sex Offense Laws - Advocates for fair and effective laws and policies related to sex offender registration and management. They offer resources and support for individuals and families impacted by sex offender registration laws: https://narsol.org/

National Association of Criminal Defense Lawyers - Provides resources and support for individuals and families impacted by the criminal justice system, including those who have engaged in sexually inappropriate behavior: https://www.nacdl.org/

National Association of Criminal Defense Lawyers. (n.d.). Collateral consequences of sex offender registration. https://www.nacdl.org/research/sex-offender-registries/

National Association of Juvenile Correctional Agencies - Provides resources and support for professionals and organizations working with justice-involved youth, including those who have engaged in sexually inappropriate behavior: https://www.najca.org/

National Association of School Psychologists - Provides resources and support for educators and families on a range of mental health and behavioral issues, including sexual behavior problems in children and adolescents: https://www.nasponline.org/

National Association of Social Workers - Offers resources and support for social workers and families working with at-risk youth, including those who have engaged in sexually harmful behaviors: https://www.socialworkers.org/

National Association of Trauma-Informed Care - Offers resources and support for professionals and organizations on how to provide trauma-informed care for individuals and families impacted by trauma: https://natcic.org/

National Association of Youth Courts - Provides resources and support for youth courts and their members, including those who are addressing sexually inappropriate behavior: https://www.youthcourt.net/

National Center for Missing and Exploited Children - Offers resources and support for families and professionals working to prevent and respond to cases of child abduction, sexual exploitation, and child sexual abuse: https://www.missingkids.org/

National Center on the Sexual Behavior of Youth - Offers research and resources on sexual behavior problems in children and adolescents, including prevention and intervention strategies: https://www.ncsby.org/

National Center on Substance Abuse and Child Welfare - Provides resources and support for families and professionals working with substance abuse and child welfare-related issues, including those impacted by sexual abuse: https://www.ncsacw.samhsa.gov/

National Children's Alliance - Provides resources and support for families and professionals working with child abuse-related issues, including child sexual abuse: https://www.nationalchildrensalliance.org/

National Child Traumatic Stress Network. (2015). A family guide to sexual abuse prevention. https://www.nctsn.org/sites/default/files/resources//family_guide_to_csa.pdf

National Coalition Against Domestic Violence - Offers resources and support for individuals and families impacted by domestic violence, including those impacted by sexual violence: https://ncadv.org/

National Conference of State Legislatures. (2022). Sex offender registration and notification laws. https://www.ncsl.org/research/civil-and-criminal-justice/sex-offender-registration-and-notification-laws.aspx

National Council on Crime and Delinquency - Provides resources and support for families and professionals working with justice-involved youth, including those who have engaged in sexually harmful behaviors: https://www.nccdglobal.org/

National Council on Family Relations - Offers resources and support for families and professionals working with family-related issues, including promoting healthy sexuality and boundaries: https://www.ncfr.org/

National Council on Independent Living - Advocates for the rights of individuals with disabilities and offers resources and support for families and professionals working with individuals with disabilities who have engaged in sexually inappropriate behavior: https://www.ncil.org/

National Criminal Justice Association - Provides resources and support for professionals and families working within the criminal justice system, including those working with youth who have engaged in sexually inappropriate behavior: https://www.ncja.org/

National Criminal Justice Training Center - Provides training and resources for professionals working in the criminal justice system, including those working with youth who have engaged in sexually inappropriate behavior: https://ncjtc.fvtc.edu/

National Disability Rights Network - Advocates for the rights of individuals with disabilities and offers resources and support for families and professionals working with individuals with disabilities who have engaged in sexually inappropriate behavior: https://www.ndrn.org/

National Gang Center - Provides resources and support for professionals and organizations working with gang-involved youth, including those who may be at increased risk for engaging in sexually inappropriate behavior: https://www.nationalgangcenter.gov/

National Family Preservation Network - Offers resources and support for professionals working to preserve families and prevent child maltreatment, including those impacted by sexual abuse: https://www.nfpn.org/

National Immigration Law Center - Provides resources and support for immigrant families impacted by the justice system, including those who have engaged in sexually inappropriate behavior: https://www.nilc.org/

National Institute of Justice. (2010). Recidivism of juvenile sexual offenders. https://www.ncjrs.gov/pdffiles1/nij/grants/236584.pdf

National Institute of Mental Health - Offers resources and information on a range of mental health issues, including trauma and recovery: https://www.nimh.nih.gov/

National Juvenile Defender Center - Provides resources and support for defense attorneys and families working with youth in the juvenile justice system, including those who have engaged in sexually inappropriate behavior: https://njdc.info/

National Mentoring Partnership - Provides resources and support for mentors and mentees on building positive relationships and promoting positive youth development: https://www.mentoring.org/

National Organization for Victim Assistance - Provides resources and support for victims and their families, including those impacted by sexual violence: https://www.trynova.org/

National Parent Helpline - Provides support and resources for parents and caregivers on a range of parenting and family-related issues, including how to address sexual behaviors in children and adolescents: https://www.nationalparenthelpline.org/

National PTA - Provides resources and support for parents and caregivers on promoting positive child development, including healthy sexuality and boundaries: https://www.pta.org/

National Resource Center for Child Protective Services - Offers resources and support for professionals working in child protective services, including those working with children and families impacted by sexual abuse: https://nrccps.org/

National Resource Center for Youth Development - Offers resources and support for professionals and organizations working with youth, including those who have engaged in sexually inappropriate behavior: https://www.nrcyd.ou.edu/

National Runaway Safeline - Offers resources and support for youth and families experiencing runaway and homelessness, including those who may be at risk for engaging in sexually harmful behaviors: https://www.1800runaway.org/

National Service-Learning Clearinghouse - Offers resources and support for educators and youth leaders interested in incorporating service-learning into their programs: https://nylc.org/

National Sexual Assault Hotline - Provides support and resources for survivors of sexual violence and their families: https://www.rainn.org/

National Sexual Assault Resource Center - Provides resources and support for individuals and families impacted by sexual violence, including those impacted by childhood sexual abuse: https://www.nsvrc.org/

National Sexual Violence Resource Center. (2021). Preventing sexual violence in youth: A guide for parents and caregivers. https://www.nsvrc.org/sites/default/files/2021-03/Preventing-Sexual-Violence-in-Youth-A-Guide-for-Parents-and-Caregivers.pdf

National Suicide Prevention Lifeline - Provides support and resources for individuals and families impacted by suicide and suicidal thoughts, which can be a risk factor for sexually inappropriate behavior: https://suicidepreventionlifeline.org/

National Youth Advocate Program - Provides resources and support for youth and families involved in the child welfare and juvenile justice systems, including those who have engaged in sexually harmful behaviors: https://www.nyap.org/

National Youth Leadership Council - Offers resources and support for youth and adults involved in service-learning programs, which can promote prosocial behavior and reduce the risk of engaging in sexually inappropriate behavior: https://nylc.org/

National Youth Rights Association - Advocates for the rights of young people and offers resources and support for youth and families impacted by the justice system, including those who have engaged in sexually inappropriate behavior: https://www.youthrights.org/

Office of Juvenile Justice and Delinquency Prevention - Offers resources and support for professionals and organizations working with justice-involved youth, including those who have engaged in sexually inappropriate behavior: https://www.ojjdp.gov/

Parenting Safe Children - Offers resources and training for parents and caregivers on how to prevent child sexual abuse and promote healthy sexuality and boundaries: https://parentingsafechildren.com/

Planned Parenthood - Provides resources and support for individuals and families on a range of sexual and reproductive health issues, including healthy sexuality and boundaries: https://www.plannedparenthood.org/

RAINN - Rape, Abuse & Incest National Network is the largest anti-sexual violence organization in the United States. They offer resources for survivors and their families, as well as information on how to report sexual abuse and find local support services: https://www.rainn.org/

Safe Horizon - Provides support and resources for survivors of all types of violence, including sexual violence. They offer a hotline for survivors and their families to get support and information on how to access services: https://www.safehorizon.org/

Safe Touches - Offers a training program for young children on how to recognize and respond to safe and unsafe touches: https://safetouches.com/

Search Institute. (n.d.). Forty developmental assets for adolescents. https://www.search-institute.org/developmental-assets/

Stop Abuse Campaign - Advocates for preventing child sexual abuse through education, advocacy, and policy change. They offer resources and support for survivors and their families, as well as information on how to prevent child sexual abuse: https://stopabusecampaign.org/

Stop It Now! - A non-profit organization that prevents child sexual abuse through education and resources. They offer a helpline for parents and caregivers to get support and guidance on how to address sexual behaviors in children and adolescents: https://www.stopitnow.org/

Substance Abuse and Mental Health Services Administration - Offers resources and support for individuals and families impacted by substance abuse and mental health issues, which can be risk factors for sexually inappropriate behavior: https://www.samhsa.gov/

The Trevor Project - Provides support and resources for LGBTQ+ youth and their families, including those who may be at increased risk for engaging in sexually inappropriate behavior due to social isolation and stigma: https://www.thetrevorproject.org/

World Health Organization - Offers resources and support for individuals and families impacted by a range of health issues, including sexual health: https://www.who.int/

Youth First Initiative - Advocates for ending youth incarceration and promoting alternative approaches to youth justice, including those who have engaged in sexually inappropriate behavior: https://www.youthfirstinitiative.org/

YMCA - Offers after-school programs and resources for youth, including those at risk of engaging in sexually inappropriate behavior: https://www.ymca.net/

Youtube: @Tools4TeensandParents
www.sayhelp.net
www.tools4teens.net

When Your Teenager's Actions Cross the Line

www.ingramcontent.com/pod-product-compliance
Lightning Source LLC
LaVergne TN
LVHW051645080426
835511LV00016B/2495